JUAN RUIZ de ALARCÓN

by Walter Poesse

In an epoch when Spain was fashioning a national drama as distinctive to its age and culture as that of ancient Greece or England's Shakespeare, Juan Ruiz de Alarcón holds an honored place with Lope de Vega and Calderón de la Barca, its greatest exponents. As the author of *La verdad sospechosa (The Truth Suspect)*, which Pierre Corneille used as the basis of his *Le Menteur (The Liar)*, he made a significant contribution to the development of the French classical theater. Through its protagonist, Don García, this drama has had a diffusion in European literature second only to that about Don Juan *(El burlador de Sevilla* or *The Trickster of Seville)* attributed to his contemporary, Tirso de Molina. Alarcón's economy of plot, his direct and natural versification, and his clear and logical manner of developing the intrigue make of his better plays works for the theatre that are still performed with frequency.

ABOUT THE AUTHOR

The author is Professor of Spanish in the Department of Spanish and Portuguese of Indiana University, where with the exception of military service (1942-1946, 1950-1951) he has taught since 1941. He received the B.A. degree from Case-Western Reserve University, the M.A. from Washington University, and the Ph.D. from the University of California (Berkeley). He has published studies on the versification of Lope de Vega and Alarcón, contributed to the bibliographies of Lope de Vega and Calderón prepared by the Research Committee of the Comediantes (Spanish Group 3 of the MLA), and compiled a bibliography of works by and about Alarcón, of which he is currently preparing an annotated edition. He holds the rank of Colonel (retired) in the Army Reserve.

Juan Ruiz
de alarcon

TWAYNE'S WORLD AUTHORS SERIES

A Survey of the World's Literature

Sylvia E. Bowman, Indiana University

GENERAL EDITOR

SPAIN

Gerald E. Wade, Vanderbilt University

EDITOR

Juan Ruiz de Alarcón

(*TWAS* 231)

TWAYNE'S WORLD AUTHORS SERIES (TWAS)

The purpose of TWAS is to survey the major writers —novelists, dramatists, historians, poets, philosophers, and critics—of the nations of the world. Among the national literatures covered are those of Australia, Canada, China, Eastern Europe, France, Germany, Greece, India, Italy, Japan, Latin America, the Netherlands, New Zealand, Poland, Russia, Scandinavia, Spain, and the African nations, as well as Hebrew, Yiddish, and Latin Classical literatures. This survey is complemented by Twayne's United States Authors Series and English Authors Series.

The intent of each volume in these series is to present a critical-analytical study of the works of the writer; to include biographical and historical material that may be necessary for understanding, appreciation, and critical appraisal of the writer; and to present all material in clear, concise English—but not to vitiate the scholarly content of the work by doing so.

Juan Ruiz De Alarcón

By WALTER POESSE

Indiana University

Twayne Publishers, Inc.   ::   New York

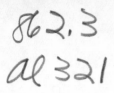
To
My Mother and the Memory
of my Father

Preface

Juan Ruiz de Alarcón[1] is ranked today, by those knowledgeable in the subject, as one of the four greatest dramatists of the Spanish *Siglo de Oro*, or Golden Age, a period of Spanish literature which reached its zenith during the first half of the seventeenth century.[2] But it has not always been so. During his lifetime he was ridiculed both for his physical deformity and for what his contemporaries thought was an unjustifiable pride. His plays were never as popular as those of others among his contemporaries, partly, perhaps, because of their more serious tone and partly because of his apparent lack of interest in writing for the theater; his slender output (small even when compared with the more modest achievements of his day) was not such as to keep his name before the public. He ceased writing long before his death and except for occasional publication and performance, his plays, and his name, disappeared from the public and literary conscience. There are probably many reasons for this, but two may be adduced here: He was born in Mexico, the only important literary figure of his day not born in Spain, even though he lived the longer and the productive part of his life in his adopted country. Although he is known only as a playwright, he was by profession and inclination a lawyer, not a dramatist. His Mexican contemporaries did not remember him, nor did he perhaps deserve to be remembered; he had contributed nothing to the Mexican literary scene. His career as a man of letters in Spain was comparatively brief and limited, being incidental to his ambition toward a different goal. Not until the nineteenth century did interest in him revive, and what we know and appreciate of Alarcón is owing in large measure to the efforts of Juan Eugenio Hartzenbusch and Luis Fernández-Guerra,[3] whose devotion to him and his works can be said to be responsible for all subsequent investigation and appreciation of the man. The impulse created by their endeavor culminated, at the approach of the tercentenary of his death (August 4, 1639), in a spate of articles and studies, including two full-length biographical-critical works as well as editions of his plays, and whereas his foreign birth had earlier been a handicap both to his own efforts and to his reputation, it now became a boon, for both the land of his birth and that of his adoption vied with each other to do him honor. His recognition now is assured and the fact that studies, dissertations, and editions have increased since the tercentenary year implies a permanence.

But although there was set in motion a new interest in Alarcón, it unfortunately came too late to find or save those data necessary for a thorough understanding and knowledge of his life, character, activities, and thoughts. Antonio Castro Leal, an admirer of the man and a student of his work, has written:

Very little is known of the private life of Alarcón. The numerous (not as numerous as one would like) documents about him of which we have knowledge are those that a man who enjoyed a scholar's pension, who obtained academic degrees, who crossed the Atlantic three times, who litigated, who sought and obtained public position, who negotiated on his own account and for others, and who, finally, disposed of his possessions when it came time to die, had of necessity to leave in public, university, and notarial archives. Of his relations with his parents we know nothing. His daughter he mentions but once: in his will. Of his friends in Spain and in Mexico, there is scarcely any mention. We do not have one single intimate document by him, not one personal letter. Of his work he wrote nothing beyond that contained in prologues of the works that he published. Of his literary life in Mexico there is not the slightest information, and of his literary life in Spain almost nothing remains but biting epigrams about his character and physical appearance.[4]

What we know of him, then, is based on a few documents, conjecture, and an interpretation of his plays. The documents are impersonal and give us little beyond a few facts; conjecture is unsatisfactory at best; and in the plays of the *Siglo de Oro* we can see a man but darkly, so difficult is it to separate personal reaction and experience from the convention to which they conformed.

The present study is an effort to present to the English-speaking reader the pertinent facts of his life, such as we have them, to

discuss his relatively meager output, and to render a critical judgment on both the plays and the technique with which they were
composed. It also endeavors to reevaluate certain opinions of his
work which have become somewhat stereotyped: his classicism,
his moral approach, his "Mexicanism," and the pronounced difference between his works and those of his contemporaries.

All citations from Alarcón's plays are taken from the excellent
edition of Agustín Millares Carlo, *Obras completas,* in three volumes (México: Fondo de Cultura Económica, 1957, 1968), which
will be cited in the text as "Millares Carlo." Where the Spanish
original has seemed unduly long, only the English translation has
been included. All translations are those of the author. The ab-
breviation BAE refers to the *Biblioteca de Autores Españoles,* or
Collection of Spanish Authors. For consistency, the Spanish form
of all proper names has been retained (that is, Juan for John,
Felipe for Philip, Sevilla for Seville), as well as certain words
relating to the drama of the time (*dama, galán, gracioso*) and
the designations of strophes.[5]

I wish here to record my gratitude to Mrs. Naomi Lawlis, Mrs.
Gail Mathews, Mrs. Emma Simonson, and Mrs. Mary Walker of
the Indiana University Library for the graciousness and expediency with which they have handled numerous requests not only
in the preparation of this work, but in my pursuit of Alarconiana
for other purposes. I am especially grateful to Dr. John C. Dowling, Chairman of the Department of Spanish and Portuguese, for
permitting me a reduced teaching load and for furnishing several
data from Spain. I owe a special word of thanks to Indiana University for a summer research grant and for funds for typing, to
Señor Miguel Bordonau, director of the Archivo Histórico de
Protocoles, Madrid, for a note relating to Alarcón, and to Señor
Manuel Uribe M., of the library of the University of Nuevo León,
Monterrey, for sending me a typescript of two articles from an
otherwise inaccessible journal. To Dr. Gerald E. Wade, editor
of this series, I cannot sufficiently express my appreciation for his
patience and for his invaluable help and suggestions.

W.P.

Contents

Contents

Chronology

1572   March 9: Alarcón's parents married in the cathedral, Mexico City.

ca. 1575   Pedro, his older brother, born in Taxco.

ca. 1581   Juan Ruiz de Alarcón born in Mexico City.

1596   June: Juan begins the course in Canon Law at the Royal Pontifical University of Mexico.

1598   August: He completes three courses in Canon Law.

1599   May 5: He completes the fourth course in Canon Law.

1600   April 11: He appears to prove that he has read "ten lessons" for the degree of *bachiller* (bachelor). April 15: He completes the fifth course in Canon Law and departs for Spain from San Juan de Ulúa in August. October 18: He matriculates in the fifth course of Canon Law at the University of Salamanca and on October 25 receives the bachelor's degree in Canon Law. On the same day, he matriculates in Civil Law.

1602   September 3: In Sevilla, he signs a receipt for the payment of 1,650 *reales* for his education left by the will of Gaspar Ruiz de Montoya. December 3: He receives the degree of Bachelor of Civil Law at the University of Salamanca.

1604   October 24: He matriculates in Laws.

1605   He completes the studies necessary for the licentiate in both Civil and Canon Law.

1606   July 4: He attends the *fiesta* at San Juan de Alfarache near Sevilla and recites some *décimas*.

1607   He is received as advocate in the *Audiencia* (Court) of Sevilla. May 25: He petitions to return to Mexico with one servant.

1608   April 12: He presents, with witnesses, a petition to be permitted to return home. It is granted, and he sails with his servant, Lorenzo de Morales, on June 3, arriving in Veracruz on August 19.

1609   February 21: He is granted the degree of *licenciado* in both Civil and Canon Law by the Royal and Pontifical University of Mexico. He seeks the degree of doctor, but asks to be excused from the expensive attending ceremonies in view of his poverty. March 12: The dispensation is granted. He seeks the chair of Institutes, but either withdraws or receives no votes. November: He seeks the chair of Decree Law, but loses to Dr. Cristóbal del Hierro Guerrero.

1610–   He pleads in the Royal Court and is legal adviser to
1613   the *corregidor* (mayor), Don Garci López del Espinar, judging and passing sentence in his place, particularly in matters concerning the traffic in *pulque*.

1611   June 11: He appears as witness for Don Francisco Santarén de Bribiesca.

1612   The court names him investigating judge in Veracruz in order to look into the facts of the slaying of Isabel Zubiri by her husband, Alonso.

1613   He seeks the temporary chair of Canon Law but loses to Dr. Pedro Garcés del Portillo. He seeks the temporary chair of Institutes, but loses to his friend, Brición Díez Cruzate. With his brother, Pedro, he begins proceedings to get compensation for the service of their parents to the Crown in the mines of Taxco. February 21: Pedro gives him power of attorney. He sails for Spain.

1614   He settles in Madrid by April 24.

1616   July 17: Juan de Grajales, impresario, agrees to pay him 500 *reales*, probably for a play.

1617   His play, *Las paredes oyen* (*The Walls Have Ears*), is performed with María de Córdoba as Doña Ana.

1618   February 3: *Los favores del mundo* (*The Favors of the World*) is presented by Baltasar de Pinedo in the convent of *Los Premostratenses*.

1622   He collaborates in the composition of the *comedia, Algunas hazañas del marqués de Cañete* (*Some Deeds of the Marqués de Cañete*).

1623   The *Elogio descriptivo* (*Descriptive Panegyric*) is published. December 14: Première of *El Anticristo* (*The Antichrist*).

1625   He directs a petition to the King for a position "worthy of his merits." June 19: The King presents the petition to the Royal Council of the Indies for further information.

1626   June 17: He is named *Relator interino* (interim Court Reporter) of the Royal Council of the Indies.

1628   The *Primera Parte* (*First Volume*) of his *comedias* is published in Madrid.

1633   June 13: He is appointed *Relator propietario* (Permanent Court Reporter) of the Royal Council of the Indies.

1634   He publishes the *Segunda Parte* (*Second Volume*) of his *comedias* in Barcelona.

1635   March 2: He presents a petition to have a seat on one of the courts of the Indies.

1639   August 1: He prepares his last will. August 4: He dies in his house on Las Urosas Street, and is buried in the parochial church of San Sebastián.

CHAPTER 1

Life of Alarcón

I In Mexico

DON Juan Ruiz de Alarcón y Mendoza was born probably in 1581 in the city of Mexico, apparently one, perhaps the third, of five brothers. His parents were Pedro Ruiz de Alarcón and Doña Leonor de Mendoza. Both Alarcón and Mendoza are distinguished names in Spanish history, and although there is little sufficiently definite to connect Juan Ruiz de Alarcón with the genteel families that bore them, it seems quite probable, in view of his later pride in his heritage and ancestry, that he was related to members of this illustrious lineage. That his parents were people of importance, at least in Mexico, is indicated by the presence at their wedding of such personages as the brother and the son of the Viceroy.[1]

On November 30, 1177, Ferrán Martínez de Ceballos, a native of Asturias, had led the attack that resulted in the capture from the Moors of the fortress of Alarcón, near Cuenca. In gratitude, the King, Alfonso VIII, named Martínez de Ceballos permanent warden of the castle and permitted him to add the name of Alarcón to his own. His son was Rui Fernández de Alarcón and later, in the thirteenth century, his descendants took the name Ruiz de Alarcón as the family name in order to be distinguished from those of the younger brothers of Rui Fernández.[2] The poet's maternal grandfather is the first of the family known to have come to the New World, possibly in the suite of the Viceroy Antonio de Mendoza, sent by Carlos V in 1535. His maternal grandmother may have been related to the same Viceroy and to the Mendoza family which has contributed so much to Spanish letters. In any case she was addressed as "Doña Leonor" and is said to have been a "noble and important" lady. Her parents were established in Taxco prior to 1572, and here, apparently, the newly-married couple settled. Although he is referred to as a *minero* (miner), it

17

is more likely that Pedro was a sort of overseer or official of the mines. Their eldest son, Pedro, and perhaps the second, Gaspar, were born here, but the mines of Taxco, which had been discovered toward the end of 1532, were becoming exhausted by 1581,[3] and the Ruiz de Alarcón family apparently moved to Mexico City before Juan was born.

Of Alarcón's boyhood nothing is known. By June of 1596, he was attending the Royal and Pontifical University of Mexico, and by April 15, 1600, had completed the five courses in Canon Law.[4] Then, for reasons unknown, he left Mexico to attend the University of Salamanca. It may be conjectured as to why he should have done so: Although all of his brothers attended the University of Mexico and two of them, at least, seem to have shown promise, Juan was the only one not interested in theology, but rather in the law.[5] He was moreover deformed, being severely hunchbacked, and since a relative had left a sum of money for the purpose of helping a member of the family through college, Juan was a proper choice.[6] He left for Spain in the flagship of General Juan Gutiérrez de Garibay, which sailed from the fortress of San Juan de Ulúa in August, 1600.

II *The First Journey to Spain*

Once in Spain, Alarcón must have proceeded to Salamanca without delay, for on October 18 his name was entered in the register as a student in Canon Law, fifth year. A mere week later, having already given proof of his knowledge of the subject, he received his bachelor's degree in Canon Law (October 25, 1600) and immediately enrolled for his bachelor's degree in Civil Law.[7]

Before and during the years of Alarcón's attendance, the number of students at the University was above five thousand, of all ages from fourteen to over thirty, and of all social classes, many of whom came "without any desire to learn and who do not study a word" and in general caused a great deal of trouble for professors and townspeople alike. The literature of the time makes frequent reference to the penniless, disrespectful, and ingenious student of Salamanca, but whether Alarcón was one of these is not documented. Fernández-Guerra (p. 13) thought that he was a conscientious and studious scholar, and Jiménez Rueda (p. 58), that he would not take part in the student escapades because of his stooped figure and his timidity, but regardless of whether he did, he seems to have been aware of what went on as the words and action of his play, *La cueva de Salamanca* (*The Cave of Salamanca*) suggest. He seems to have liked Salamanca. Not once in his works does he make reference to the University of Mexico or to his life there, but in the same play (vv. 661–64) he speaks of Salamanca as "this University, where wise Minerva now has her sacred cult, of which Athens is jealous" (*En esta Universidad,/ donde la sabia Minerva/hoy tiene el sagrado culto/de que está celosa Atenas*).

Alarcón received his bachelor's degree in Civil Law on December 3, 1602, and continued his studies for the licentiate. These were concluded June 24, 1605, but he did not receive the degree. "The taking of the degree of bachelor was a comparatively simple and inexpensive affair, without great ceremony, but it was otherwise with the degrees of licentiate and doctor. . . . Owing to the great expense [these degrees] were not frequent at Salamanca."[8] In view of the number of times that Alarcón pleaded poverty, the expense involved could well be the reason that he did not take the degree.

III *In Sevilla*

From Salamanca, Alarcón returned to Sevilla, possibly for one or all of three reasons: It had been the home of the deceased relative whose munificence apparently had enabled Alarcón to attend the university; it was a prosperous and growing city because of the trade with the New World and thus the scene of much litigation, a fertile field for a fledgling lawyer; it was the port from which he would sail for his return to Mexico.[9] Schons (p. 64) concludes that he arrived in Sevilla toward the beginning of 1606, for on July 4 of this year he took part in a *fiesta* which was celebrated in the *huerta*, or estate, *San Juan de Alfarache*, belonging to an alderman, Don Diego Colindres, and located on the right bank of the Guadalquivir.[10]

The part taken by Alarcón in the *fiesta* is an interesting one, showing an aspect of his character not to be found elsewhere. Early in the morning of the fourth, the participants left Sevilla by boat and proceeded to the estate. Breakfast was at ten; at two there began the *certamen*, or poetic contest, in which twelve poets took part. Alarcón's contribution was a series of four *décimas* (the *décima* is a ten-line poem) preceded by an explanatory or apolo-

getic *redondilla* (quatrain) addressed to a lady who was in distress because her hands perspired profusely, the gist of which is
that since the hands that were perspiring were of a lady such as
she, the perspiration was nectar worthy of the gods. "The author
was very pleased upon hearing his *décimas* read, *as if they were
good* [italics added], in view of which it was declared that, since
he [the author] must have perspired more in writing them than
did the lady whose perspiration gave rise to them, said lady
should be obliged to perspire with her author to even
things, . . ." [11]

There came near the sound of a loud whistle and it caused all to be
attentive until they saw issuing from one side of the patio a courier,
the cause of this noise, and behind him a muffled person of less than
medium stature. They came on two horses, or rather, the horses came
on them, since they were of the type that are used in the dances of
Corpus Christi Day [that is, they were cardboard horses]. In this manner they made a hasty turn around the patio and went out through
another door, this adventure leaving astonished the ladies leaning out
of the upper portion of the court as well as the gentlemen spectators
in the lower portions. . . . [Later] there were heard shouts that the
Prince of Chunga[12] (Juan Ruiz de Alarcón by another name) was
approaching to joust and he was the person in disguise who made the
entrance on the horse that I have mentioned. Desirous of knowing this
new adventurer, we all turned our faces at the time that he entered in
the patio prancing, with arms of cardboard the color of iron, with gold
relief; the plume of his helmet was a handful of reeds as green as those
that have just been cut; his breeches were of yellow paper, with slashes
[or slits] of the same, although red, with various embroidery made of
it and of the finest and most resplendent tinsel that ever Flanders has
produced or Germany seen; . . . He jousted with the aide of the
officer presiding over the contest and with such good spirit did both
perform that they came out rewarded with two pairs of gloves. The
adventurer presented his to a veiled lady, and the aide to himself, giving way to another tourney.[13]

Alarcón was to become embittered and discouraged, but in 1606
youth and hope were still with him. He was then about twenty-
three.

Although he did not receive the degree of licentiate before leaving Salamanca, he was permitted to practice law in Sevilla and
early in 1607 was received as a lawyer in the *Audiencia* (Court or

Tribunal) of Sevilla.[14] In May, he petitioned to be permitted to leave Spain "not being one of those prohibited from going to those kingdoms [the New World]" and to take with him one servant. His intention was to serve in the employ of the Bishop of New Cáceres in the Philippines, Fray Pedro Godínez Maldonado, apparently, thereby, being able to make the voyage more cheaply, but the plans went for naught because the ships that were to make up the fleet were requisitioned by the Spanish government to combat Dutch pirates who were then menacing the coast of the country.[15]

IV *The Return to Mexico*

On the twelfth of April of the following year, Alarcón again petitioned to return to Mexico where "I have my home, mother, and brothers; I came from there eight years ago to Salamanca to study and [ask permission] because of having finished my studies and not being married or one of those forbidden." [16] Since he had mentioned his parents in the petition of the previous year, he had possibly received notice of the death of his father in the meantime. Although he had earlier sought to take three servants, when granted permission to leave the following month, he was allowed only one, Lorenzo de Morales, who accompanied him "as secretary and servant." [17] He sailed in the flagship, "Diego Garcés," of a fleet of more than seventy ships under the command of Don Lope Díez Aux y Armendáriz whom he was later to praise in a *comedia*. Among the passengers were Fray García Guerra, later viceroy and Alarcón's patron, and Mateo Alemán, the author of *Guzmán de Alfarache*. The fleet left Cádiz on June 12, 1608, and arrived at San Juan de Ulúa on the nineteenth of the following August, eight years to the month after his departure from Mexico.[18]

Since he had not received the degree of licentiate at the University of Salamanca, Alarcón now sought it from the University of Mexico. During the first part of February of 1609, he offered testimony of his studies in Spain, presenting a thesis, a copy of which is still in existence in the archives of the National Library of Mexico. He was successful in its defense and was granted the degree of licentiate on Febuary 21

so that in all of the realms of the King, our lord, he may be so called, enjoying the exemptions and liberties which by reason of the said degree should be reserved to him, and permission is granted to him that whenever he might wish and according to his will, he may receive the degree of doctor in the said faculty of law, . . . and the said licentiate giving thanks, the said ceremony was completed . . .[19]

Alarcón did wish to receive the degree of doctor and on March 12, only twenty days later, he petitioned to be granted the degree *sin pompa* (without ceremony), being "as poor as is evident to your lordship." Permission to dispense with the ceremony, which was an expensive affair and paid for by the candidate himself, was granted for this and other "just reasons and motives and its being the period of Lent." [20] But there is no record of his actually receiving the degree.

At first Alarcón may have been attracted by the academic life. Later in the year, there occurred a vacancy in the chair of Institutes and among the competitors was Alarcón, but when the vote was finally taken, in September, he had either withdrawn his candidacy or received no votes whatsoever. Later, an opportunity arose to compete for the newly vacated chair of Decree Law, but in the balloting of November 9 Alarcón came in last of five candidates, with only nine votes to the forty-nine of the winner.[21]

Having failed to obtain a university post, Alarcón turned to the practice of the law whose study he had been pursuing for more than ten years. Many years later, in 1635, when seeking a seat in one of the courts of the Indies, Alarcón made a statement of his experience, in which he gives a summary of his activities during this period.[22] In 1611, Don Garci López del Espinar, the *corregidor* or mayor of Mexico, who had come in 1606 as an appointee of Felipe III, commissioned Alarcón to act for him in the suits brought against those making *pulque* and selling it to the Indians. For years the government had been trying to suppress the practice in order to stamp out the "vice of drunkenness" among the natives, without, as might be expected, much success. Alarcón's duties consisted of visiting the places where the *pulque* was made or sold, seizing the effects of the owners, initiating suit against them, and bringing them before the *corregidor*, with whom he sat in judgment. Once the sentence was pronounced, it was his duty to see that it was carried out. When López del Espinar had to be absent from the city, he reconfirmed Alarcón's commission in order that during the interim he might hear by himself all of the suits that "had been or might be filed" during this period, and, Alarcón adds modestly, "in the *Residencia* (municipal building) he was considered a good judge."

The duties of a *corregidor* were not only to attend the municipal council meetings (*cabildos*), but also to serve as judge of civil and criminal suits. He was permitted to have as aides an *alcalde* (justice of the peace) who would help in ordinary matters, so that the *corregidor* could attend sessions of the Council, and a lieutenant, who could discharge the *corregidor*'s duties in his absence. López del Espinar wanted to be excused from appointing a lieutenant and, in fact, was absent from the city only twice in his six-year term and then for short periods, but he did, apparently, desire or require a legal aide. A document of 1625 refers to Alarcón as having been a *teniente de corregidor* (mayor's aide), but officially he seems never to have had the title. With or without it, he served as *letrado y asesor* (lawyer and advisor) to López del Espinar and enjoyed his trust, since in the following year "the said *corregidor* gave him the same commission in order to ascertain and sentence with it."

Besides these duties, Alarcón practiced his profession before the *audiencia* (court) of Mexico and in the same year of 1611, was given a special assignment. According to the laws pertaining to the Indies, the *audiencia* could commission judges for matters outside of their district. They were to serve only in very serious cases, to gather information, and to turn over their findings to the *audiencia*, where the case would terminate. The *audiencia*, therefore, sent him as investigating judge to Veracruz, where, some time before, a certain Ginez Alonso, public notary, had dispatched his wife "by stabbing," apparently with accomplices, and the father of the lady was demanding justice against him "and the other culprits." Alarcón was to hear the several parties and then pronounce sentence "according to the law and justice." Unfortunately, we do not know what his decision was, but having made it, "he turned it over to the *audiencia*" for review.[23]

Alarcón still maintained an interest in the university, however. On November 13, 1611, his friend Bricián Díez Cruzate, who had been a student with him in Salamanca, served as witness for him in Mexico, and competed with him for the chair of Institutes, received his doctor's degree. As part of the ceremony, there was a *vejamen* (vexation), or criticism, remarks "made 'with wit and grace,' saying ridiculous things, but taking care 'not to slander or say anything that might wound or hurt feelings, but only that it come to vex or criticize the candidate, in conformity with the use and practice common in worthy universities.' And for the said *vejamen* the candidate will pay twenty *pesos* and no more." Unfortunately, this document has disappeared. It would be interesting to know how Alarcón amused his audience without offending his friend.[24]

With Brición he again competed for a university chair, this time for the temporary one of Canon Law, in April, 1613. Both lost out, but he tried again later in the year for the temporary chair of Institutes. Alarcón's petition for this chair is extant. In spite of his previous failures, he laid down certain conditions, among them that he be allowed two hours free in the morning and again in the afternoon to attend to his own business. He also requested that the balloting be done in secret. Not only did Brición receive the largest number of votes, but Alarcón did not get even one.[25]

As Jiménez Rueda says (p. 108), 1613 was a year of trial for Alarcón. He had failed completely to obtain a university position and the term of office of the *corregidor* under whom he was serving was about to end. His friend, the Viceroy, Don Luis de Velasco, had returned to Spain in 1611 to assume the presidency of the Council of the Indies, and the possibility of getting an appointment to the Council may have occurred to him. His mother had died, since in this year he refers to those who "had been" his parents.[26] So far as is known he had not married and was thus free to move about.

V   The Second Voyage to Spain

These developments may have made easier his decision to return to Spain for the purpose of furthering the careers of himself and his elder brother, Pedro, or the brothers may have decided to take advantage of the opportunity that Juan's return to Spain offered to their advancement. The decision was made at least as early as February 21, 1613, the date on which Pedro granted a power-of-attorney "as may be required by law to the licentiate Juan Ruiz de Alarcón Mendoça, my brother, generally in order that in all my suits . . . he may recover all . . . that may be owing to me and will be owing . . . and that he may seek recompense before the King, our lord, and his Royal Council of the

Indies for my services and merits . . ." [27] Laden with transcripts as to his brother's character and with the triple purpose of improving his brother's lot, advancing his own career, and seeking recompense for what the brothers thought had been insufficient monetary recognition of the contribution that their family had made to the royal treasury while serving the king in the mines of Taxco, Alarcón left Mexico sometime between May, 1613, when he was still seeking a university position, and November 15, 1613, when a witness testified that he was then "in the kingdom of Castile." [28] By April 24, 1614, he had settled in Madrid,[29] to experience a different existence, and to live out the remainder of his life.

The man of letters had not yet appeared.[30] Except for his contribution to the *fiesta* at *San Juan de Alfarache* and a laudatory *décima*, written prior to 1611, perhaps as a student in Salamanca, he seems not to have given any thought to literary writing. Fernández-Guerra (p. 475) has him sketching a play on the ship returning him to Mexico in 1608, and Castro Leal (p. 37) asserts with great confidence but with no accompanying evidence, that "upon arriving in Madrid, in 1613, he carried in his luggage some *comedias*, five or six, those that he had written in Salamanca, Sevilla, or Mexico," and (p. 73) that 'it can be asserted that he began to write for the theater by 1601, in Salamanca." Hartzenbusch attributes three plays to him before 1599,[31] but there is really no indication that he was writing plays or even giving any consideration to the theater at this time. He had studied for the law, had devoted himself to legal practice and to seeking university chairs in law, and was now concerned with litigation and getting a government post. He was about thirty-three years of age at the beginning of his pursuit of office in Spain, which was to be his chief occupation, and of an apparently reluctant literary career, which, alone, was to bring him lasting fame. This fact has its own touch of irony.

In 1614, it had been only eight years since Madrid had been reestablished as the capital for the last time. Although some effort was made at building, paving, and urbanization, the city, down to the beginning of the eighteenth century "remained a badly-built, dirty, and unhealthy place." [32] Nevertheless, it must have had its pleasant aspects, for the writers of the period, including Alarcón, speak fondly of the scene of the court. To it came nearly all of the great men of letters and the arts and it was here and in this period that these aspects of culture flourished as never before or since. Of Madrid Alarcón has his characters remark: "A beautiful town! The best; all [others, compared] with it are villages." Hernando, one of the characters, adds that in his six years of wandering the globe, he has never seen any beauty more rare, even though, in the same play he makes reference to its unpleasant odors. Alarcón could also be critical of the city, particularly of the people and of the court, with its extravangance and its corruption, but he never abandoned it, and it was to be the scene of his remaining activities, literary and otherwise. Of his twenty authentic plays, eight take place wholly or in part in Madrid.

For several years he seems to have occupied himself with Pedro's business, for there is record of his having received money sent by his brother. Whether through Juan's efforts or his own "merits," Pedro succeeded when Juan did not; in 1656, some seventeen years after Juan's death, he was still holding the posts that he had received.[33] The relationship between the two brothers then fades into the obscurity that surrounds that of Alarcón with the other Mexican members of his immediate family, not one of whom he mentions in his will of 1639.

VI   Poet and Playwright

It was not long before Alarcón became acquainted not only with the great men of letters of the time, but also with the intrigue, backbiting, and frustration of the court. What the source of his income was is not clear. It is probable that he practiced his lawyer's profession. It is certain that he continued to seek a government post, but in this he was to have no success until 1626, and then only partially. It is possible that Pedro sent him money from time to time.[34] What he achieved in the matter of compensation for the services of his father is not known. In any case, there is little doubt that he suffered from poverty, or at least, what he considered poverty, in view of the frequent, and bitter, references to *pobreza*, or poverty, in his plays. Equally bitter are some of his references to *pretender* (jobseeking). To tide him over, as it were, he resorted to writing plays. Dramatic writing was perhaps the most lucrative of all genres. Lope, too, tells us that he wrote plays only for the money, and Alarcón mentions that they brought six hundred *reales* each when sold to a producer.[35]

In spite of the conjectures noted above of an earlier start,

Alarcón seems not to have begun his dramatic career until after settling in Madrid, or about 1615, and ended it about ten years later.[36] He, himself, tells us that "these eight *comedias* [of the first volume of those he published], then, if not licit diversions of idleness, virtuous effects of the need in which the delay of my pretensions placed me, may your Excellency receive in his protection" and "with you [the *vulgo*, or common people] I speak, wild beast . . . take these *comedias;* treat them as you are accustomed, not as is just, but as is your pleasure, for they behold you with scorn and without fear. . . . If they displease you, I shall rejoice to know that they are good, and if not, it will avenge me to know that neither is the money that they are to cost you," and again addressing the reader, this time in his second volume of plays, he writes, "whoever you may be, whether dissatisfied or of good intention, know that the eight *comedias* of my first volume and the twelve of this second are all mine, although some have been the feathers of other crows . . ." These are not the words of a man who took pleasure in writing for the theater, who wrote *comedias* over a long period, who wrote prolifically, or who tried to ingratiate himself with the public. He admits that he wrote them for income and that he was mainly concerned with his *pretensiones* (jobseeking). His specific mention of "eight" and "twelve" implies that he wrote no others. Indeed, it was more usual for a volume to contain twelve plays. Had he written more than eight when the first volume was prepared for publication, in or before 1622, would they not have been included?

It seems strange that this urge toward writing plays should suddenly develop and flower. One would assume some reputation for him as a poet, some expressed liking for the theater, even though there were many, and often of little talent, who tried their hand at composing *comedias* during this era. Of his poetry prior to 1615, there are extant only fifty-four lines of what is scarcely more than versifying. Nevertheless, that Alarcón soon established himself in the literary circles of the capital is manifest in the enmity and ridicule that he aroused among his contemporaries. His plays, his appearance and character, and his pretensions, both to a position and to gentility, his assumption at this time of the title *don,* all came under attack. An obscure and insignificant man would not have been a suitable target for such verbal assaults as he received.

By the end of 1621, Alarcón had written at least the eight

comedias which he gathered together to be published in the first
of two volumes of his dramatic works, since on January 29 of the
following year Antonio Mira de Amescua, a fellow dramatist,
signed his approval of the publication of these plays, observing
that there was in them "much moral and political doctrine worthy
of the genius and letters of the author," but the volume was not to
appear until six years later.

The next year Alarcón accepted a request of Luis Belmonte
Bermúdez to collaborate with him and seven others in writing a
play about the exploits of Don García Hurtado de Mendoza, the
fourth Marquis of Cañete, whose part in quelling the revolt of the
Araucanian Indians of Chile in 1557, according to his son, had not
received sufficient attention in an epic poem, *La Araucana,* by
Alonso Ercilla y Zúñiga. Among the nine collaborators were such
distinguished dramatists as Luis Vélez de Guevara, Antonio Mira
de Amescua, and Guillén de Castro. The play was printed in 1622
in a special edition, in which Alarcón's name was listed along with
those of the other collaborators, and was performed at least twice,
apparently in the apartments of the Queen, between October 5,
1622 and February 8, 1623. Although the play has little literary
merit and adds nothing to the reputation of any of the contributors, the circumstances of its composition indicate that Alarcón
was known as a dramatist and poet.[37] His next collaboration, however, was disastrous.

VII   *The Descriptive Panegyric*

In 1623, the Prince of Wales, Charles Stuart, destined to be
Charles I of England, came to Madrid for the purpose of explor-
ing the possibility of marriage with the Princess María, sister of
Felipe IV. The dazzling prospect of thus bringing together two of
Europe's most powerful nations which had been at sword's point
during most of the hundred years that had elapsed since another
Spanish princess had married a Prince of Wales evoked an extravagant reception and entertainment that reached its culmination in
August. Among the participants was the Duke of Cea, scion of
one of the most influential and noble houses of the time. He was
appointed *mantenedor* (presiding official) of a contest planned,
and, desirous of perpetuating the event, the Duke asked Alarcón
to compose an *Elogio descriptivo* (*Descriptive Panegyric*).
Alarcón was not the facile, extravagant poet that the occasion re-

quired and he yielded to the suggestion of Mira de Amescua that he parcel out the task, as had been done with the play about the Marquis of Cañete, gather the parts together, work them into a unified poem, and present it to the Duke. The result was a composition of seventy-three octaves offered with the statement: "Descriptive Panegyric for the festivities which His Majesty Felipe IV held in person in Madrid, August 21, 1623, in celebration of the agreements between his Serene Highness Charles Stuart, Prince of England, and her Serene Highness María of Austria, Princess of Castile. To the duke, governor [of Castile, etc.]. He who errs in obeying, does not become unworthy in erring; in this trust this composition dares to come to the hands of your Excellency and in one [the trust] he does not fear the other [the hands]. May our Lord keep your Excellency. The licentiate Don Juan Ruiz de Alarcón y Mendoza." [38]

An ultra-euphuistic attempt to portray the procession and subsequent contest or mock skirmish that formed part of the celebration, the poem is full of mythological allusions and other extravagances and is now of worth and interest only because of the storm which it brought forth around the head of the luckless Alarcón. An anonymous critic prepared a copy for the Count of Monterrey on which he made 113 annotations of a sarcastic nature, but before it could be sent, he learned not only that the stanzas were not by Alarcón, but also who had contributed and how many, and that Alarcón had asked for them "in the style of Don Luis [de Góngora]" and arranged them. This the commentator found hard to believe "as much because of not being able to persuade myself that our poet would do such a thing, as because the octaves are so bad." Upon investigation, he learned that it was true and that those who contributed had done so in order to make fun of Alarcón. Whether their intent at first was to embarrass him or whether this was a way out when they beheld the result, their action was reprehensible, but Alarcón's part, if we are to believe his contemporaries, was hardly more honorable. Not only had he not named his collaborators in presenting the work, but he apparently received money for it which he did not share with them. In a fury, the participants and others loosed their grievance upon him in a shower of *décimas* of a very abusive character, some of them comparing the deformed character of the poem with the physical deformity of the target of their barbs.[39] He was even summoned to appear before his accusers in order to hear these *décimas* and to answer the charges, but he did not attend.[40]

The year 1623 was to have one more unpleasant episode for him. On December 14, there occurred the first performance of his play *El Anticristo* (*The Antichrist*), probably written not long before, a performance which ended in utter failure for the play and confusion for the audience. An enemy of Alarcón placed a flask of foul-smelling liquid in the patio and the odor drove the audience out and even caused some to faint. Order apparently restored, the leading actor was so unnerved that he refused to make the required flight through the air at the end of the play, whereupon the leading lady (who, in her part, had fallen dead offstage) seized the crown and mantle of the actor "coupled to the ring of the rope the iron hooks of the flying jacket that she was wearing" and completed the act.[41]

VIII   *Interim Court Reporter*

During this period, Alarcón had not ceased pursuing his goal of obtaining a governmental position, and in July of 1625 he addressed a memorial or petition to the King in which he mentions that for twelve years he has been "pretending" or seeking a governmental post and desires to be employed in a position "worthy of his letters and profession." The King ordered the Royal Council to investigate his qualifications and merits and make an account of them as well as the way in which he might be employed in the service of his Majesty. The reply was a résumé of his experience, with a reference to the contribution of his parents and grandparents to the royal estate and the frank statement that although worthy in talent, he was unacceptable because of his "bodily defect." Instead, it was recommended that he be given some lesser post, such as court reporter of one of the Councils.[42] The following year, June 17, 1626, he was offered the position of *relator interino* (supernumerary or interim court reporter) on the *Consejo Real de Las Indias* or Royal Council for the Indies, with the right to be the first to be considered when a vacancy as *relator* arose.[43]

The duties of the Council were considerable. Practically all of the matters which had to do with the Indies were resolved by it: political, such as the provision of viceroys and courts; financial, such as the taxes owing to the King in different branches of commerce and industry; permits to colonize and settle; organization; inspection; departure of the fleets that periodically set sail from Sevilla; review in the second instance of important civil acts which had been judged, in the first instance, in distant kingdoms. The *relator* had to prepare the information and opinions which the councilors later endorsed, attend to the directions which they gave him in order that the resolutions be adapted to the jurisprudence of the Council and the desires of the King.[44] Having received a post which apparently furnished him a comfortable living, Alarcón turned his back upon the theater.

IX   *The Final Years*

The permanent appointment for which Alarcón was the first to be considered did not occur until the year 1633, on June 13 of which he was made *relator en propiedad*. After this he appears to have settled into a life of comfort, if not affluence. He rented a house on Urosas Street (*Calle de las Urosas*), acquired a coach, a coachman, and both a manservant and a maidservant. Certain "fringe benefits" also attended the position, including the rental for his house, expenses at Christmas (*la ayuda de costa de Navidad*) and "certain and definite fees" (*ciertas y determinadas propinas*). And if he had money to spend he also had it to lend, his will listing no fewer than six people who were his debtors.[45]

Having achieved the security that he had so long desired, Alarcón limited his literary activity to the composition of occasional verse by way of observing some new work or event and the publication of the second volume of his *comedias*. The approvals for the last had been granted in 1633 and it was printed in Barcelona in 1634. It is not clear why he decided to publish his plays, nearly ten years after their composition, but one may conjecture that he was annoyed because some of his works had been *plumas de otras cornejas* (feathers of other jackdaws).[46] Still bitter and sarcastic, he addressed himself to the reader, putting the blame for improper attribution on the publishers "who give them to those they wish and not to the authors to whom they have been attributed, whose greater indifference does more than my greatest vigilance; and so I have wanted to declare this, more for their honor than for mine, for it is not right that their fame suffer because of the marks of my ignorance." This volume, like the first, is dedicated to Don

Ramiro Felipe de Guzmán, the president of the Council for the
Indies, and perhaps Alarcón thus desired to show his appreciation
for both the original appointment and his recent "promotion."

Jiménez Rueda (p. 295) gives an imaginative account of his life
during these years which might very well be within the limits of
the probable:

Alarcón is an author who was a friend of order. In his daily life he
must have been methodical also, orderly, exact, precise. We can imagine him coming out of his house on Urosas Street early, setting out for
the Council to dispatch the business of which he had charge with scrupulous meticulousness, returning then to his house in order to eat what
his servant, María Benita, had cooked for him. Nap for half an hour,
study, alone, some intricate problem of his profession, in order to give,
on the following day, an opinion adapted to right or to the political
expediency of the moment. In late afternoon to go for a walk or a ride
in his coach which his coachman, Gregorio Sánchez, had duly readied
for him. Some friend probably accompanied him, his Council mate,
Don Antonio de León Pinelo, for example, or the agent of the same
body, Don Gaspar de Deybar, or Captain Bartolomé Gómez Reynoso.
After a frugal supper, he perhaps received the visits of his friends, that
of a nephew of his, Don García de Buedo, that of a lady who is named
as a niece of his, Doña Magdalena de Silva y Girón. His servant, Mateo
Díaz, would have his bed ready and he would get into it before the
temperature became too cold. . . .

Still he was not satisfied. He continued to hanker after the position which he had thought should be his ever since he had come
back to Spain, a position in one of the courts of America. In 1635,
he addressed another petition to his Majesty, or, more probably,
the same memorial that he had been presenting periodically, asking for a seat on one of the courts of the Indies.[47] Once more he
was unsuccessful.

Sometime during the year of 1637 he fell ill. He began to absent
himself from the sessions of the Council and it was necessary to
appoint in his place a *relator interino,* who entirely replaced Alarcón in the beginning of 1639. On the first of August of this year he
prepared his will, outlining in detail his burial and memorial ar-
rangements, directing the collection of debts owing to him and
the payment of those he owed, making bequests to his servants,
niece, and nephew, and leaving the bulk of his estate to his natu-

ral daughter, Doña Lorença de Alarcón, then the wife of Fernando Girón and living in a small village of La Mancha. On the fourth of August he died. He was not yet sixty.

When Lope de Vega died, a few days short of four years before, he was given a funeral that was both elaborate and impressive, the ceremony lasting nine days.[48] No account remains to us of the obsequies that attended the death of Alarcón. According to his will he was buried in the parish church of San Sebastián, not far from where Lope had been interred in 1635.[49]

If the terms of the will were carried out, the crosses of the parish with all of its priests accompanied the body, and a mass was sung either at that time or on the day following the funeral with all of the priests in attendance. Nine days later another mass was sung with the same priests attending. Finally, he directed that five hundred masses be said for the repose of his soul and those of his parents and "other persons to whom I have obligation." [50]

Lope's death occasioned many eulogies, which were gathered together and published by his friend, Pérez de Montalbán, who in turn was similarly honored when he died in 1638, but even in death Alarcón was not free of the unkind remarks that had accompanied him throughout his life. José Pellicer de Tovar, less than a week after his passing, wrote: "There has died Don Juan de Alarcón, a poet famous as much for his *comedias* as for his hunchback, the *relator* of the Council of the Indies." [51]

X *Evaluation*

What manner of man was Alarcón? We have only the most meager of clues as to his character and his private life. No known portrait is extant,[52] but according to his contemporaries he was of medium stature, with a red beard and, probably, red hair. He was noticeably misshapen, his deformity being prominent humps both in the chest and in the back, which never ceased to arouse the amusement, and scorn, of his contemporaries, to one of whom is attributed the remark that from a distance it was impossible to determine whether he was coming or going. Quevedo describes him as having spindle legs, and other contemporaries refer to his foul breath. In all, he could not have made a very attractive appearance.[53] His biographers, among them Fernández-Guerra, Jiménez Rueda, and Castro Leal, picture him, in general, as a retiring individual, hurt by the cruel jokes hurled at him, cringing in loneliness and discouragement, a strong defender of moral correctness and uprightness. He could not have been insensitive or insensible to the barbs that were flung at him, but he was not above replying in kind. Among those who mocked him was Cristóbal Suárez de Figueroa, who, in a work first published in 1617, made fun of his assuming the title of *don* and adding to his name that of his mother, *Mendoza.* Suárez was notorious for his biting tongue and malevolence[54] and Alarcón retaliated in his play *Las paredes oyen* (*The Walls Have Ears*) by having the servant, Beltrán, gleefully remark that there is in the capital a slanderer so vicious that if he were to be burned at the stake, everyone would rush to bring the firewood (vv. 2293 *et seq.*).

It is very difficult, in the *comedia,* to separate what an author wishes to present as part of the convention of the genre and what are his own thoughts and opinions. Nevertheless, perhaps more in the works of Alarcón than in those of his more famous contemporaries, it is possible to discern something of the author's character. The *comedia* was designed to please the audience and the audience called the tune, but Alarcón, more aloof from the public and less disposed to placate it, was more inclined to express his own opinions. Thus we notice that he is preoccupied with his *pobreza* (poverty), *pretender* (seeking a government post), and *nobleza* (gentility) and the lack of recognition the last received. Frequently we read such laments as "pressed, God knows, by hostile poverty," or "Sir, if you would be rich, change your name from Don Juan to Justino or Federico, for cruel fortune has ever hated the noble," or "in my courage and nobility, it were no crime to love her, but being poor, I need the favor of his Highness to attain her." To Alarcón, poverty was especially bitter because it obscured in the eyes of others, he thought, what was noble in a person, whether of ancestry or of character.

With the same insistence, Alarcón plays upon the theme of seeking a position in the capital: "I received permission and came to Madrid to seek a post," or "my [evil] fortune has now achieved its intent, since my long *pretensión* [jobseeking] has brought me to such a state that I can no longer keep the servants that I once did." In his play, *La prueba de las promesas* (*The Test of Promises*), Alarcón has a scene, extraneous to the plot, in which three jobseekers are being interviewed. The third, inquiring about his petition, is told that he must show his valor if he wishes to be a captain. "But is not my presence and bearing sufficient?" he queries, and is advised that "his Excellency has horses of better appearance." The petitioner then promises a reward of a thousand doubloons if his petition is favorably received and is immediately granted what he wishes (vv. 2547 *et seq.*).

The man who emerges, then, although not too distinctly, from his plays and what is known of him is one who labored under enormous physical and psychological handicaps, who was not insensitive to ridicule, but was able to stand up to it and even answer it,[55] not permitting it to deter him from either his goal or his desires. He possessed a sense of humor, if one somewhat more restrained than that of his contemporaries. He was persistent, if not shameless, in his quest for a government sinecure. He had a touch of the complainer, was preoccupied with money, or the lack of it, and took great pride in himself and his ancestry. His part in the *Descriptive Panegyric,* an illegitimate daughter, and satiric references to him as a lover[56] cast a shadow on his character, but we do not know all of the circumstances. He wanted most of all security and, having achieved it, he was satisfied to live a quiet life of comfort, abandoning the career to which he had made a real contribution and through which his name has come down to posterity.

CHAPTER 2

Comedias *of the* Primera Parte
(First Volume)

I *The* Comedia *as a Genre*

ALARCÓN'S place in Spanish literary history is owing solely to his contribution to the drama. Unlike many of his contemporaries, he wrote neither profusely nor in other genres. His incidental poetry is scanty both in quantity and in quality, and if he composed any legal writings, they have disappeared. The genre that Alarcón essayed is peculiar to Spain and to an era. In brief it was a play which might be comic, serious, or even (though rarely) tragic, composed in three acts and in a variety of strophes. Regardless of tone or theme, it was called a *comedia*.[1] The subject matter was equally varied, historical and imaginative, religious and profane. The author usually showed his ingenuity in the development of the plot rather than in characterization, and the chief themes, repeated ad infinitum but with variations, are honor, friendship, loyalty to one's lord, love, jealousy, and vengeance. The usual means by which the intrigue became more and more involved are mistaken identity, deception, eavesdropping, fabrication, disguises, and misunderstanding. The nature of the genre led usually to an abrupt and often illogical denouement.

II *Chronology and Classification*

It is not possible, with our meager knowledge, to establish with any degree of certainty the dates of the composition of Alarcón's plays, nor the order in which they were written. Several chronologies have been proposed, from that of Hartzenbusch, who spreads the plays from around 1599 to the 1630's, to that of Professor Courtney Bruerton, who proposes as the earliest date, 1613, and the latest, 1625, limiting himself to the authentic plays. Bruerton's seems the most satisfactory, but owing to the fact that any chronology is conjecture, the plays will be discussed in the order in which Alarcón himself published them, in 1628 and 1634, respectively, followed by those attributed to him.[2]

Equally unsatisfactory are attempts to classify them. Professor A. V. Ebersole divides them into works of love intrigue (*enredo amoroso*), semitragedies, plays using magic, one religious play, and one of honor and vengeance. Ludwig Pfandl classifies them as dramas of ideas, historical dramas, dramas of fantasy, and dramas of society, with four subdivisions under dramas of ideas.[3] It is not easy to compartmentalize *comedias,* and those of Alarcón are no exception, since the elements that predominate in one type are to be found in various degrees in the others as well. The majority (13) of those of Alarcón are *comedias* of contemporary times, even though they may be set in earlier periods, may include historical personages, or even, as in *El desdichado en fingir* (*The Unlucky Feigner*), be set in a foreign land. Five plays are based on historical or semihistorical events, one, *El Anticristo* (*The Antichrist*), can be classified as a religious play, and one a play of romantic adventure, *El tejedor de Segovia* (*The Weaver of Segovia*), although Pfandl considers the last a historical drama. There are magic episodes in one of the contemporary plays, in one of the semihistorical plays, and in the religious play, and although Professor Ebersole lists *The Weaver of Segovia* as the only play of honor and vengeance, two of the historical plays are also of this character.

III   Los favores del mundo (The Favors of the World)

This play is both the first and the longest of those that Alarcón himself published. Bruerton assigns it to 1616?–1617. The title reflects rather Alarcón's own attitude toward a "world" in which he was failing to receive what he expected and thought his due, and which seemed to prefer wealth and manipulation to nobility of person and character. At least twice he has a character comment that the lucky wins out over the honorable (vv. 624–25, 2268). A more appropriate title would be "The Whims of a Capricious Prince," since it is the instability of Prince Enrique that causes the changes in fortune of the protagonist, rather than the "world." The play had been completed and performed by 1618, for on February 10 of that year, the impresario, Baltasar de Pinedo, "confessed" that he had presented it, along with *Las paredes oyen*

(*The Walls Have Ears*) in the main chapel of the convent of Our
Lady of Victory (*Nuestra Señora de la Victoria*), an event that
resulted in a scandal.[4]

Fernández-Guerra (p. 270) cites a document in which Enrique
III (died 1406), in return for services rendered to his father, Juan
I (died 1390), presented to one Garci-Ruiz de Alarcón the town
of "Villanueva, which is near the river Júcar, one league from your
town of Buenache," all in the province of Cuenca, scene of the
early activities of the Alarcón family, and he adds, significantly, a
"tradition" to the effect that having an enemy in his power, Garci-
Rüiz pardoned him when he heard him exclaim "May the most
Holy Virgin help me!" Alarcón substituted for Enrique III his
grandson, Enrique IV (died 1474). Since the Prince did not assume the throne until 1454, when he was twenty-nine, the date of
the action is sometime before this.[5] But the time and place are
really Madrid of 1614–1618, for the characters speak of fine
houses, coaches, and the *comedia*. Besides a royal prince, Alarcón
has retained only the person of Garci-Ruiz and the episode of the
pardon, and about them he has woven an intricate plot in which
one lady, Julia, plots, and nearly manages, to thwart the love
affair of Garci-Rüiz and another lady, Anarda, who has several
suitors, among them, but with less than honorable intention, Enrique. Only a reading of the play can give a true idea of its in-
volvement, the humor of its *gracioso*, and the characters of the
main personages.

Critics have had high words of praise for the piece,[6] and it is, in
fact, a well-constructed work, particularly in the manner in which
Alarcón has each "up" followed by a "down" of Garci-Rüiz' fortune and in the portrayal of some of the characters. Its weakness
lies in its excessive length, with a tendency toward diffuseness.

The two main characters do not live up to the promise of the
beginning. Garci-Rüiz is typical of the "hero" of the *comedia*, fear-
less of his enemies, jealous guardian of his honor, a vassal loyal to
the point of obsequiousness, at least for a modern, and sickeningly
abject in his love. For a man famed for having fought against the
Moors and one who has hunted for six years to clear his honor, he
becomes almost demoralized at every downward turn of his fortune and, as one editor remarks, his refusal to accept the hand of
Anarda unless his prince consents is *poco sincero . . . y poco
galante* (not very sincere or gallant),[7] but he becomes a person of

stature when he refuses to go along with Julia in her evil plot. Anarda's aggressiveness in pursuing her love for Garci-Rüiz and her defiance of her uncle when he tries to force a marriage upon her contrast with the ease with which she falls for Julia's intrigues. "You are only my uncle," she had said, "and not even my father can rightly force my will: marriage and religion are to be at my pleasure":

> *Vos no sois más que mi tío,*
> *y ni aun mi padre en razón*
> *puede forzar mi albedrío:*
> *casamiento y religión*
> *han de ser a gusto mío.* (vv. 1718–22)

More consistent are the other important characters. Julia is the personification of meanness, "one of the most disagreeable figures in Alarcón's theater," a "repulsive character." [8] The prince is a curious mixture of nobility and a spoiled child.

One incident is usually singled out for comment in any discussion of the play, that in which Garci-Rüiz pardons his enemy, Don Juan, when the latter calls upon the Virgin. For example, Barja writes that "Alarcón was not one of those who thought that every question of honor was to be settled by killing the offender," [9] but the scene can hardly be cited as an example of Alarcón's humanity or of his opposition to the exacting of vengeance. Alarcón was using a tradition, Juan's remark is more of an exclamation of dismay at his fall than a true plea to the Virgin (he was, moreover, innocent of Garci-Rüiz' charges) and Garci-Rüiz reacted more from superstitious fear than real devotion; as Professor MacCurdy points out,[10] most of the Golden Age dramatists avoid bloodshed in their cape-and-sword plays. Alarcón, in three later plays, has a man run through over a matter of honor, even though in our play he has the prince expatiate on how much better it is to pardon *after* the offender has been rendered helpless than to kill him.

IV   La industria y la suerte (Intrigue and Luck)

This play, whose title might also be translated as *Ingenuity and Luck* or *Intrigue versus Luck*, is similar in theme to its predecessor and to several works to follow: the difficulty that an individual, poor but of honorable birth, has in his struggle against the world with its wealth and its concern with the superficial. So far as can be determined, the plot is Alarcón's own invention and he introduces no historical personages. The composition of the play has been placed anywhere from 1601, because of the references to Sevilla (with which Alarcón was probably acquainted as early as 1600), to 1621, the date of the death of Felipe III of whom mention is made (vv. 806–10) as being alive. Bruerton sets the date of composition as 1620–1621. The scene of the action is Sevilla and the time contemporary with Alarcón.[11]

Two *galanes*, Arnesto, newly rich, unscrupulous, and cowardly, and Juan, noble but poor, love Doña Blanca, or at least her money; she prefers Juan. Earlier Juan had encouraged and then rejected another lady, Sol, who plans revenge. The plot revolves about the intrigues of Arnesto and Sol to break up the affair between Blanca and Juan, but in their zeal they compromise each other and, according to *comedia* convention, have to marry, a fate each richly deserves. Thus, by means of luck (*suerte*) Juan and Blanca win out over the machinations (*industria*) of their respective rivals.

Jiménez Rueda thinks (p. 162) that it is a "nice" (*linda*) *comedia*, but Castro Leal (p. 104) comments on its contrived character (*mecanismo*). In spite of this and its rather unsympathetic characters, the action is more tightly controlled than in *The Favors of the World* and there are several scenes of both dramatic and humorous effect. One is that in which Juan loses a note which is cleverly, if unethically, recovered by Arnesto's servant; in another a servant, Agüero, debates with himself whether to deliver a note written by Sol. In still another, Agüero, having been bribed by Juan to deliver a note to Blanca, loses his nerve. Instead he slips it into a book which she has requested. Finding the note, Blanca composes an answer, but on the same type of paper and sealed in the same way as the original. She then summons the trembling Agüero, sternly reprimands him for his forwardness, and orders him to return the "unopened" note to the sender, but Juan, thinking that it is indeed his own being returned, fails to read it. There is also one that was to suggest scenes in at least two later plays (*Las paredes oyen* and *La amistad castigada*, or *Friendship Punished*). It occurs between Sol and Nuño, the latter a brother to Blanca, a superfluous character of the work but in love with Sol. She, tired of his importunities, tells him that if he really loves her there is something that he can do for her. He jumps to seize the opportunity of pleasing his lady, but is crest-fallen when she tells him that this favor is to leave her alone, and to keep out of her sight, "for much persistence wearies pleasure and bores love . . . desire increases with deprivation, so, while I behold you I neither need you nor sigh for you":

> *que la mucha porfía*
> *el gusto cansa y el amor hastía*
>
> . . . .
>
> *que con la privación crece el deseo,*
> *y así, mientras te miro,*
> *ni me haces falta ni por ti suspiro.*
>   (vv. 2099–2100, 2104–06)

There is greater motivation in the activities of Arnesto and Sol than in those of the other characters. The former, in his ambition for wealth and influence, is not about to brook opposition; the latter is angered because Juan has abandoned her, chiefly because she has not come into money as he expected. Blanca is more ag-gressive and less gullible than Anarda of the previous play. Juan is typical of several Alarconian *galanes*, complaining of his poverty and because fortune seems to favor his rival, yet brave when fac-ing a male opponent, generous in his treatment of a fallen enemy, honest and honorable, but like Garci-Rüiz and many others, he is successful, not because of his own drive so much as because the intrigues of his opponent have failed. His treatment of Sol, how-ever, is less than gallant. The loss of her expected inheritance forced him, he says, "to change, if not my love, my intent," and "if you can, do the same, for if you wish to, you are a woman, and you will be able to":

> *si no el amor, el intento.*
>
> . . . .
>
> *si pudieres,*
> *haz lo mismo, que si quieres,*
> *mujer eres, y podrás.* (vv. 484, 490–92)

V   Las paredes oyen (The Walls Have Ears)

Perhaps the second best-known work of its author and one of the jewels of the theater of the *Siglo de Oro*, this play differs from the two just discussed and the general run of *comedias* in that the victorious *galán* is not only poor and luckless, but also deformed and homely. In this character, appropriately called Don Juan de Mendoza, Alarcón is undoubtedly portraying himself, and wishes to "prove" that nobility of family and soul should triumph over wealth, handsomeness, and a mean spirit. The title, based on a *refrán*, or proverb, seems to have inspired the play rather than the play, the title. There are several variants: "The walls have ears and the mountains, eyes"; "the walls have ears and eyes"; "the walls have eyes at times"; and "the walls hear." The plot appears to be Alarcón's own.[12]

The character of the slanderer, Don Mendo, according to Fernández-Guerra (p. 255), is based on those of Góngora, the Count of Villamediana, and Suárez de Figueroa, all well known for their mordant tongues, but as Castro Leal points out (p. 124), there was no need for a specific model "to create a type that abounds in the world." It also has been considered an answer to the vicious comments of Cristóbal Suárez de Figueroa in his *El pasagero* (*The Passerby*) which was published in Madrid in 1617.[13] Its action is contemporary with its date of composition, and it takes place in Madrid and the nearby university town of Alcalá de Henares.

The plot is relatively simple, the complications arising from misunderstandings and duplicity. Don Juan de Mendoza is hopelessly in love with Doña Ana, a young and pretty widow, but she gives him no encouragement, being interested solely in the handsome and dashing Don Mendo, over whom all the women rave. He has already won the heart of Teodora and Lucrecia, and he does not discourage their hopes since he believes in having a "spare," a lady to whom he can turn should the first object of his wooing fail him. But Mendo has a great fault: he is given to making slanderous and unkind remarks about people. Unfortunately for him, he slurs the beauty and character of Doña Ana, unaware that she has overheard him. Ironically, Mendo, for once, does not mean what he says; his purpose is to discourage the potential rivalry of a newly-arrived duke. Since others have heard this slander, Doña Ana can no longer honorably accept Mendo, and when she confronts him with his words he tries to lie out of them. Eventually, desperate at the thought of losing her, he attempts to kidnap her, an attempt which is aborted by Juan. This act of Juan, his thoughtfulness, and his patience are rewarded when Ana transfers her affections to him.

The play has some weaknesses. One is the break in time in the first act, part of which takes place before Ana's departure for Alcalá and the remainder a week later, after her return to Madrid. A more serious defect would appear to be the insufficiently motivated change of heart on the part of Ana. One can understand her rejection of Mendo, but the change from her positive dislike for Juan to her eagerness to marry him seems a little implausible. She justifies this by saying that beginning to cease to dislike is the beginning of loving. Moreover, she is obligated to Juan for both his verbal and his physical defense of her, and obligation is a major force in the *comedia*. But the weaknesses fade before the general excellence of the work, its rapid and direct action, its sparkling dialogue, and the delineation of its characters.

Doña Ana is a young widow wanting to remarry, a woman naturally attracted to a handsome man, considerate of her servants, and careful of her reputation. Yet she can be unfeeling, and one of the best scenes in the play is the exchange between her and Juan: He wishes to be alone with her in order to deliver a letter, but when the servants have left, he tells Doña Ana that *he* is the letter and proceeds to declare his love. Finally Doña Ana asks, "Do you want anything else?"

DON JUAN	What more besides you?
	If you wish to understand my state,
	it is written in the fact that I love you.
DOÑA ANA	Well, then, Don Juan, good-bye.
DON JUAN	Wait: Won't you answer me?
	Do you leave me this way?
DOÑA ANA	Have you not told me that you love me?
DON JUAN	I have and you can see it.
DOÑA ANA	Did you not say that your intent
	was not to ask me to love you
	because it would be too daring?
DON JUAN	So I have said and that is what I feel,
DOÑA ANA	Have you not said that you have
	no hope of winning me over?
DON JUAN	That is what I said.
DOÑA ANA	And that you are unable
	to equal me in worth,
	did your tongue not assert this?

DON JUAN I said it in that way.
DOÑA ANA Well if *you* have said it all,
        what do you want me to say? (vv. 285–304)

Doña Lucrecia, the second *dama*, is something of a snoop and a tattletale, but lacks the mean streak of the rival *damas* of the two earlier plays. She is clever enough to see through Mendo and to reject him when she can have him. She has a fine moment toward the beginning with an unnamed count, whom she eventually accepts. Mendo wants the count to justify him before Lucrecia's accusations and expects him to lie for him, but after he leaves, the count, really in love with Lucrecia and hoping that Mendo will remove himself by marrying Ana, tells Lucrecia the truth and she replies:

> What intrigues are you inventing? Be silent!
> Could Don Mendo say such a thing?
> Do you seek thus to get me
> to be grateful for your affection?
> Do you think that I am going to love you
> even if I should hate Don Mendo?
>
> (*¿Qué enredos inventas? ¡Calla!*
> *¿Tal pudo decir don Mendo?*
> *¿Que tu afición agradezca*
> *quieres así disponer?*
> *¿Piensas que te he de querer,*
> *aunque a don Mendo aborrezca?*) (vv. 662–67)

Two other characters who play large roles but contribute little to the plot are the servants, respectively, of Ana and Juan. That of Ana is Celia, probably the most admirable of all the female servants in Alarcón's works. She sees the good qualities in Juan and advances his suit, but whereas other maids advance the cause of the *galán* as a result of bribery, Celia does it from conviction; there is no evidence that Juan tries to influence her in any way other than being kind and considerate. She is also clever and sagacious, being able to observe human character more acutely than her mistress, Ana. Beltrán is a faithful, wise, and learned companion for Don Juan, and alternately chides and encourages his master in his apparently hopeless love.

VI   El semejante a sí mismo (The Resembler of Himself)

With this *comedia* (another title of which might be *His Own Impostor*), we come to a type of play more like those of Alarcón's contemporaries, Lope and Tirso; that is, a work in which the protagonists intrigue in order that their love may triumph, with less dependence on the workings of fate through the failure of the minor or "bad" characters to succeed. The *galán* takes a more aggressive role and there is an almost independent secondary plot, which concerns itself with another pair of lovers. Each couple has its own affair and does not seek to disrupt that of the other. At the same time, their activities involve one another so that we have a more complicated, if a more contrived, play, a true comedy, the type that must have delighted the audiences of the day. The use of disguise, mistaken identity, impersonation, reappearance of people who have disappeared or been thought dead, coincidence, were all favorite ingredients of the popular play, and here they are in good measure.

Fernández-Guerra (p. 174), followed by Henríquez Ureña[14] and Castro Leal (p. 96), thought that Alarcón's inspiration was "El curioso impertinente" ("The Persistently Curious Fellow"), a *novelita* or short story that Cervantes inserted as Chapters XXXIII and XXXIV of the first part of *Don Quixote* (1605), in which a man is so intent upon testing his wife's fidelity that he forces on her his friend, to the eventual besmirching of his own honor and ultimately his death. But the similarity is rather tenuous. In the play, Juan invents an imposture to prevent being separated from his beloved and he does not put her fidelity to such a dangerous test.

The action is set in Sevilla at a time contemporary with its date of composition, which Bruerton thought to be 1614–1616.[15] Don Rodrigo has given a home to his niece, Ana, since the death of her father makes him the next in the family to look after her honor and thus that of the family. Juan, Rodrigo's son, has fallen in love with Ana, and Rodrigo, for reasons of his own, orders Juan to Peru to look after some family interests. To avoid this threatened absence, Juan concocts a daring and improbable plan. He will impersonate a cousin in Madrid, Diego, whom the family has never seen, and come to Sevilla for a visit to his "uncle" thus gaining constant and unimpeded access to Ana's presence. Diego is also to come to Sevilla to act as Juan's servant. The complications that

arise from such a bold scheme form the substance of the play. The
secondary plot involves Diego and Julia, a lady whom Diego had
known years before in Flanders, but whom he believed dead. In
spite of innumerable pitfalls, Juan succeeds in carrying out the
deception and eventually wins the hand of Ana, while Diego and
Julia manage to resolve a number of misunderstandings to their
mutual satisfaction.

Fernández-Guerra (p. 174) calls the work a *comedia* of intrigue and pure entertainment, but poorly worked out, with situations that are too implausible, a scarcity of interest because of the
lack of the unity of action, and with all the defects of a "first
work." Millares Carlo (I, 295) says that it is one of the weakest of
Alarcón; Castro Leal asserts (p. 98), that it is obviously a youthful
work, although he admits that the plot is ingenious and brought to
the stage with ability. One hesitates to contradict such eminent
authorities, but given the purpose and nature of the *comedia* and
the plot that Alarcón has chosen to develop, it is very well done.
The unlikely intrigue has been worked out with great skill. The
main characters are more vigorous and aggressive than many of
those of the preceding plays, and for once we have a *galán* who is
ready and willing, even at considerable risk, to do something to
further his love affair. Although his motive, love, is justifiable, his
disobedience is not, and he is made to suffer for it by the gnawing
realization that it is "Diego" and not Juan that Ana seems to love.
The preciseness of Alarcón's legally conditioned mind is apparent
in the careful preparations made by Juan to deceive his family
and to make the improbable as plausible as possible. Although
Diego is a party to the deception, he is, on the whole, a more admirable person than Juan, but quite unreasonable in expecting Julia
to have remained faithful to him after having long since lost con-
tact. Both of the *damas* are among the better sketched and more
likeable of those of Alarcón. Ana is a spirited, independent, and
consistent creature, unimpressed by Juan's jealousy, and Julia, if
somewhat petulant, lacks the meanness of her namesake in *The
Favors of the World*. Sancho, the servant of Juan, and the *gracioso* of the play, has a role out of proportion to his importance.
One has the impression that he is there more to amuse the audience and express the author's ideas than to serve his master. He is
more buffoonish than the *graciosos* whom we have already met,
much less in the confidence of his master, and less trustworthy.

His characterization may be conditioned by the fact that Juan needed Diego at his side to serve as his "servant, Mendo."

The play moves rapidly in spite of two long and really irrelevant descriptions, respectively, of the drainage activities in Mexico and the departure of the ship from Cádiz, but the audience of the time apparently enjoyed this type of declamation; it attended the theater to hear as well as to see and descriptions of activities foreign to the experience of most could not have failed to impress it. The time that elapses has to encompass the departure of a minor character, Leonardo, his being swept overboard, his rescue, and his return to Sevilla, but the play moves right along and this, with what Castro Leal (p. 99) says is an "argument developed in effective and well-combined situations," does not permit either of the two plots to become frayed, or the suspense to sag, for even though separate, they logically and easily join and part from each other as the action proceeds.

VII   La cueva de Salamanca (The Cave of Salamanca)

Black magic with other aspects of the supernatural has always had a fascination for men, the dramatists of the *Siglo de Oro* among them, and this play is Alarcón's first of several treatments of the subject.[16] It is a curious hodgepodge of elements, which Alarcón has introduced in one way or another, not altogether satisfactorily. It portrays student life in Salamanca, his only play set in the city in which he had spent the years 1600–1605, and it is, as well, a drama with a *dama* and *galanes*. To all of this he has added the ingredient of magic in the activities of two personages apparently based on historical characters, one of whom, the Marqués de Villena, famous as a magician, Alarcón seeks to vindicate.

Although the Moorish cities of Toledo, Córdoba, and Sevilla had long been associated with the magic arts, Salamanca, in the sixteenth century, began to rival and then to overshadow them, perhaps because of the renown of its university, which was becoming recognized as one of the great institutions of learning in Europe. The so-called "cave" of Salamanca, to which frequent mention is made, has never been adequately identified, which is not surprising since its characteristics were probably a transfer of those of the legendary cave of Toledo, but the existence of such a cave had a firm hold in the minds and literature of the sixteenth and seventeenth centuries. One tradition was that the devil taught black magic in the cave, accepting seven new pupils each year, one of whom had to agree to remain with him when the year was up. Another was that one student, in order to escape, tricked the devil by leaving his shadow in his place.

Among the legendary figures of Spanish literature is Enrique de Villena, known, although incorrectly, as the Marqués de Villena (1384–1434). His preference for study instead of arms, for seclusion instead of the attractions of the court, his vast learning and his gift for languages, his compositions and comments on the supernatural and matters of magic, and the eventual destruction of part of his library by order of Juan II as works going beyond the bounds sanctioned by the church, gave rise to his reputation as a practitioner of necromancy, a reputation that increased with the passing of time, even though his contemporaries do not mention it. Among the legends that arose was the one in which he had himself cut into pieces and pickled in a bottle so as to return to life later, and another, that he was the one who tricked the devil by leaving behind his shadow. Alarcón for reasons of his own seeks to vindicate the marquis by disproving such stories, and to do so he includes as a character a Marqués de Villena who is a descendant, possibly the son, of the famous Enrique, another bit of legend since Villena left no sons. It is the "descendant" who seeks to explain the legends concerning his ancestor.[17]

The other character of possible historical antecedent is Enrico, "a serious old man and student," who is the real magician of the play and to whom Villena comes for instruction. Fernández-Guerra (p. 131) identifies him as Enrico Martínez (d. 1632), a Dutchman, who was educated in Spain, enjoyed the title of royal cosmographer, wrote and published books, and supervised the construction of the tunnel for the *desagüe* (drainage) described in *The Man Who Resembled Himself*. Alarcón may have known him in Mexico and been impressed by his accomplishments and learning.[18]

The jumble that resulted from Alarcón's efforts to incorporate so many elements, the play's change of direction in mid-action, and its apparent lack of purpose, have led some critics to assume that it was an early, youthful work. Hartzenbusch (p. 518) thought that it was written for performance while Alarcón was still a student in Salamanca, but one argument against this is the reference

to Madrid as the capital, whereas Valladolid was the residence of
the King from 1601 to 1606, when Alarcón was in Salamanca.
Waxman (p. 400) calls it "an amateurish piece of student work."
Castro Leal (pp. 93–94) thinks it an early work but "extensively
revised" upon his return to Spain; if so, one can only wonder what
the original was like. Fernández-Guerra (p. 172) thought it one
that Alarcón had been carrying around in his *cofre* (trunk) and
finally extracted and revised. Bruerton gives the dates 1617–1620,
but with question marks.

The play has little literary merit. The comic, almost slapstick,
early scenes of student life give way to a disagreeable scene just
short of rape and to tiresome arguments about the practice of
black magic. The major interest lies in the picture of student extra-
curricular activities and in the play's being the first of the Villena
cycle.[19] It is of interest also because of what it tells of Alarcón's
preoccupation with the supernatural. Lest any one (the authorities in particular) get the impression that he believed in it or ad-
vocated it, he seeks to rationalize some of the things that had
been rumored about the "cave." In the play it is no longer a cave,
but the windowless house of Enrico. The bronze head (*cabeza de
bronce*) which Villena is rumored to have had is really the
learned mind of Enrico. In the end, Enrico admits that black
magic is wrong and acknowledges the error of his ways after a
rather weak defense against an investigator sent by the king. Finally, the young Marqués de Villena seeks to justify his ancestor
(or father) by saying that although the devil was expecting him
in hell as a result of his diabolical practices, he repented in time
and, deceiving the devil, gave rise to the story of the shadow; the
bottle or flask tradition resulted from there being enclosed in a
small tomb such *grandeza* (greatness).

It is, then, a disjointed play, a series of episodes rather than a
well-developed plot. The result is that there are some good scenes
and portrayals, but the work as a whole is mediocre and the characterization, weak. The student scene at the beginning is well done
and even amusing in spite of its brutality. Two lively scenes, although the second borders on poor taste, are given us when Clara
resists the advances of her impetuous *galán*, Diego. She is truly in
love with him, but not so much so that she fails to keep in mind
her honor; she insists on marriage before intercourse. She rejects
the love of García, Diego's companion, because, like Lucrecia in

The Walls Have Ears, she thinks it disloyal for a man to make love to the lady courted by his friend.

VIII   Mudarse por mejorarse (Changing for the Better)

The title of this play is difficult to translate succinctly and implies a loftier intent than is actually the case. Although it means "to change one's mind so as to improve oneself," the interpretation in the play is "to change one's mind so as to improve (selfishly or as a matter of expediency) one's lot." Alarcón varies the usual by having the two *damas* as aunt and niece. The latter is not much younger or more beautiful than the former and the plot consists mainly of the efforts (not exactly laudable) of the suitor of the aunt to shift his attentions to the niece when the latter comes to Madrid. It represents Alarcón in one of his more lighthearted moments. There is one reference to the *comedia* and its audiences and others to Suárez de Figueroa or another of the evil tongue, but Alarcón refrains from complaints on poverty and on the failure of others to recognize what is worthy.

If it is true that Alarcón is referring to Suárez de Figueroa (vv. 1647 *et seq.*), his remarks may well be (as in *The Walls Have Ears*) an answer to the biting sarcasm that Suárez made in his work, *El pasagero,* published in 1617, thus suggesting as a date for the play either that year or the following. Both Castro Leal (p. 129) and Bruerton propose a date around 1618. The time is that contemporary with Alarcón and the action takes place in the capital, Madrid. The situation is comparatively uninvolved and concerns the difficulties that arise when García falls in love with Leonor and courts her while keeping her aunt, Clara, unsuspecting. Eventually Leonor, who was originally and momentarily interested in him, rejects him in favor of a marquis. Clara, none the wiser, accepts the fickle García when he returns to her.

The apparent simplicity of the main plot is enlivened by the series of intrigues and complications that are required before García learns his lesson. It is well organized, moves forward rapidly, and the uncertainty of the outcome is maintained nearly to the end. In addition it is spiced with numerous delightful scenes, observations, remarks, and interesting characterizations. At their first meeting (Act I, Scene 4) García visits Leonor during the absence of her aunt. This disturbs the chaste Leonor and when she believes that he has come to seek her aid in his love for her aunt, she replies that she is neither old enough nor smart enough to be a go-between (*tercera* or "third party"), but when García declares that it is *she* whom he loves, she replies that, although offended at being expected to be a *tercera*, she is scandalized at being a *primera* ("first party") at the expense of her aunt. "Is it customary in Madrid?" she asks (vv. 230–32), "to love aunt and niece at the same time?" (*es uso en Madrid corriente/enamorar juntamente/a la sobrina y la tía?*). Callously, García says that he is justified in leaving the aunt for the niece, when the niece is so divine, so as to better his situation. But what about constancy? replies Leonor. Loving the best is not a proof of constant love, since no steadiness is required there, but "constant is he who scorns a more fortunate opportunity" (*firme es quien hace desprecio/de otra ocasión más dichosa*). García admits that that is being constant, but it is foolish, and Leonor replies that since he is abandoning her aunt for her, she will have to resist his love until she learns whether there is a prettier niece to replace her.

A pleasant commentary on love and courtship is to be found in Act II where the marquis tells his friend, Otavio, of his hopes with Leonor. He reveals that he has plenty of money and that all he seeks is to have at his side a sweet companion and a noble mother of his children. Otavio asks why he does not just ask for her hand since his chances are unquestionably good and the marquis replies: "How little you know of love!"

> He who begins with the (marriage) contract,
> Otavio, deprives himself of the pleasure
> of facing scorn,
> of overcoming an aloofness.
> As in the narrow-mouthed cup
> the pleasure increases in the drinking,
> so is the glory greater
> to the degree that it is more desired.
> The gambler, when he is anxious
> to see the card, does he not find
> more pleasure in uncovering it gradually
> than if he looks at it at once?
> The hunter, could he not
> at the cost of a small price,
> get the light heron,
> obtain the swift rabbit?
> But (instead) with dog and falcon

> he tires himself for greater glory,
> esteeming the victory
> more than the possession.
> Well, let me conquer
> the wild beauty
> whom I could so easily
> get by proposing. (vv. 993, 997–1020)

Although he can remedy his situation merely by asking for her hand in marriage, he prefers to "uncover gradually in the cards of her eyes the good fortune" that he is getting; he wants to make a ceremony of the love that will be born in her, the favors that she will do for him, and the flattering remarks that she will make to him. Then, suddenly shifting to the practical, he admits that she may already love someone else or even fall in love with someone equal to him. "In short, before attempting such a dangerous undertaking, taking the pulse of matters is to want them not to go wrong."

> *Y al fin, antes de intentar*
> *empresas tan peligrosas,*
> *tomar el pulso a las cosas*
> *es no querellas errar.* (vv. 1045–48)

The main characters of the play are among Alarcón's best. Don García as a person is unlikely to have any admirers other than Doña Clara. Not only does he transfer his affections with the greatest of ease, showing an insensitiveness to the feelings of a lady that is hardly gentlemanly, but underhandedly he seeks to hide from her his true intent. He deserves to lose Leonor, but Clara, a sensible and trusting lady, does not deserve *him,* nor he, her.

Leonor is a puzzling character, now clever, loyal to her aunt, and concerned with her own reputation, then on the verge of disloyalty, carrying on the intrigue with García, her aunt's suitor, attracted by the man in spite of her previous scolding of him for his inconstancy. One critic thinks that there is "nothing favorable in this frightful (*torvo*) character to rehabilitate it," but another, that she is a lady of lively talent, astute intelligence, and great practical sense.[20] She is a bewildered young lady, whose innate good sense triumphs in the end. Her reply to García that she, too, seeks to better her lot is Alarcón at his best.

Doña Clara is both astute and gullible, a paradox to be observed in many characters of the *comedia,* not only of Alarcón but of his contemporaries as well. She is undoubtedly still a young and attractive woman, since she has three admirers in the play, to Leonor's two. The marquis, Arnesto, is perhaps one of the most stable, sensible, and attractive figures that Alarcón created. The other characters are little more than figures for the manipulation of the plot. Only Redondo emerges above them, a good *gracioso* characterization, who not only is a companion to his master, but an active participant in furthering his love affair, and who amuses with his comments and observations on the court, women, and the *comedia.* A pretty but stupid woman, he says, is like a flower made of tinted paper, which is attractive when seen from afar, but worthless, because without fragrance, when brought close.[21]

IX   Todo es ventura (Everything Is Chance)

Not as well known as the preceding work, this play is an excellent example of Alarcón's ability to develop a plot from an initial misunderstanding. Again we have his preoccupation with the role of luck (*suerte*) or fortune (*ventura*), and the discouragement attending his quest for a government post, but here there is lacking the bitterness and the petulance to be seen in some earlier plays. Both Castro Leal (p. 105) and Bruerton give 1614 as the earliest date of composition, although the latter extends the possible date to 1617. Fernández-Guerra (p. 199) also chooses the date of 1614 because in April of that year "there occurred an incident which entertained *tertulias* and *corrillos* (gatherings and groups) . . . , and suggested to Alarcón the beginning of a very lovely *comedia.*" The incident was a brawl that erupted when a powerful nobleman sought to remove from the custody of two bailiffs a man whom they had arrested for having wounded a lad. Seizing the prisoner, the nobleman and his companions sought refuge in a convent. Although eventually detained and imprisoned, the offenders were soon freed. In *Everything Is Chance,* a nobleman requests the release of a prisoner by the bailiff; the latter complies with the remark that it is better to free a guilty person than to offend a great lord. The implication is that this was a not uncommon occurrence and, therefore, the play need not have been inspired by the incident of the brawl as related by Fernández-Guerra. At most, it inspired an episode in the play, not the plot itself, which seems to be Alarcón's own creation.[22] The plot consists of a series of unexpected developments which steadily improve the fortunes of an unsuspecting, undeserving, impoverished *hidalgo* (petty nobleman), Tello, who, in spite of himself, obtains the favors of his superiors and the hand of the *dama,* Leonor. There are numerous embellishments to the main plot, including a secondary intrigue, the love affair between the characters Belisa and Enrique, which is almost independent of the main theme, although interwoven with it. There are also scenes of comic effect, particularly one in which the servant, Tristán, equipped with a ludicrous disguise in order to deliver an unsigned note for Leonor, feigns a sleep which becomes real and ends with his being doused with cold water. With four *galanes* and but two *damas,* Alarcón also ends the play on an amusing note: the marquis and the duke, left out in the pairing-off, offer their hands to each other.

Although the strength of the play lies mainly in the skillful way in which each of the successive improvements in Tello's good fortune is introduced, there are in addition interesting characterizations. Leonor is a lady who knows what she wants, even though she appears misguided in her adulation of Tello. Her refusal to be distracted from her goal in spite of exile and a conniving friend give her an aggressiveness not usually found in Alarcón's women. Belisa is another of his unlovely women. Tello is unique among *galanes,* another Alarconian *galán* who is different from the general run; in fact, he is more *gracioso* than *galán.* Tristán, who at the beginning of the play promises Enrique, his poverty-stricken master, to stay with him until death, is an excellent portrayal of a *gracioso:* loyal, sometimes wise, occasionally stupid, witty, and fond of his wine.

On the whole, critics have not given much space to the play. One who has writes that it is a good play, of "great merit in thought and in execution." [23] Its neglect is unfortunate, for it is a well-conceived, cleverly-executed *comedia,* marred only by one scene (xiii of Act III) in decidedly poor taste.

X   El desdichado en fingir (The Unlucky Feigner)

The last of the *comedias* published in 1628 is unique in Alarcón's work in that it is his only imaginative *comedia de enredo* or intrigue set outside of Spain. The scene is a "city of

Bohemia," which, with Hungary and Poland, was a country that the dramatists of the time liked to use as a setting, perhaps for variety, perhaps for the exotic flavor that foreign names and lands imparted. But in spite of the scene of action and the classical names (Arseno, Persio, Ardenia) of the characters, the work is neither Arcadian nor Bohemian in any real meaning of these words. The streets and customs are those of Madrid, the actions and reactions those of the usual characters of a typical *comedia.* Castro Leal (p. 83) gives its date of composition as 1601–1603?, *"revisada posteriormente"* (later revised), a frequent, but unsubstantiated, observation of his, and it is one of the three that Fernández-Guerra (p. 172) has him carrying around for years in his trunk. Millares Carlo (I, 649) and Bruerton prefer the dates 1613–1615.

The theme is similar to that of *The Resembler of Himself,* but now it is the *dama,* rather than the *galán,* who concocts the idea of an impersonation, which results in an overload of "incidents which make it confused; each one of the stories of Persio, Arseno and Arnesto could give a theme for a work." [24] Ardenia loves Arseno, who loves her in turn, but the Prince of Bohemia also loves her (for recreational purposes only) and, as a subject, she cannot defy him by marrying Arseno immediately. It is a situation reminiscent of *The Favors of the World* and other *comedias,* wherein princes on the prowl make life difficult for the local swains. It is up to Ardenia to put off the Prince without offending him and to bring about her marriage to Arseno. She has one other suitor, Persio, who, however, has fallen in love from a distance and whom she does not know or recognize. Her plan is to have Arseno impersonate her brother, Arnesto, who went to Rome as a mere boy to accompany an uncle entering the service of a cardinal. He is to pretend a return because the uncle has died; the lapse of many years and the age of her father should permit the deception to pass. Through an intercepted note, Persio learns of the plan and it is he who comes as the impostor to the consternation of Ardenia, her family, and her lover, when the last belatedly appears as the "brother." The confused and amusing events that follow are finally resolved with the union of Ardenia and Arseno, the forced marriage of Persio with a lady, Celia, whom he had previously deceived, the return of the real brother, whose escapades in Rome add to the suspense, and the renunciation of the prince of his infatuation for Ardenia. There is a certain weakness in versification in that there are only eleven hendecasyllables in the nearly three thousand verses, but the almost exclusive use of the octosyllable is not without its effect: a rapidly moving, unabashed comedy, in which unsuspected and amusing developments and sprightly conversation leave no dull moments.

One of the finest comic scenes in Alarcón occurs in Act II when Arseno appears at the home of Celia to tell her that he now has other interests. In her fury, she snatches from him a piece of paper which Persio had handed to him as the lost note from Ardenia. Each time that Celia questions him, he tells her to read the note: "It will explain" (*El papel lo dirá*). It is a *romance* written by Persio himself, but so cleverly composed that what Celia does read seems to apply to Arseno and he becomes more and more uncomfortable. Believing that she has proven her point, Celia stops reading, but Arseno, wanting to know how it ends, seizes the paper. As *he* continues, the truth comes out that Persio once possessed and abandoned Celia and it is her turn to blush and to make excuses. The scene is too long for reproduction here, but some of the more pertinent exchanges may give an idea of it:

CELIA.   I shall read this note
          if it cost me my life.
ARSENO.   If you will leave me alone with that,
          take it and may you burn up in it.
          Did you think that it was a lady's
          note?
CELIA.   I shall see.
          (*She reads*) "Listen, friend Montano, to
          the activities of a poet:
          For six months after
          God brought me to this land
          I went about free and without worry
          when through God and luck
          I met a lady . . ."
          Arseno, what lady is this?
ARSENO.   The note will say: Read.
CELIA.   (*Reads*) "of good figure, face and attributes:
          in short, I liked her."
          And she, did she like you?
ARSENO.   The note will explain: Read.
CELIA.   (*Reads*) "I found out who she was . . ."

>   —I swear, Arseno, that you
> are not wanting in diligence—
> "and I learned that she was a maiden . . ."
> What difference does it make that she be one?
> Promise her marriage, as you did me.

ARSENO. For heaven's sake, Celia, you are a fool.
How do you know that I am the one
to whom this note refers?

CELIA.   The note will say. I shall read:
"and that her name was Celia."

ARSENO. What?

CELIA.   So now my name is bandied about
in verses, sir! Did you not see
that if I am to be your wife
it is well that I have a good name?

ARSENO. Are there no Celias besides you?

CELIA.   No, for Arseno there are no other Celias.

Although the note refers to the activities of Persio, it seems to describe what Arseno did when *he* first met Celia, including some uncomplimentary remarks about Celia's aunt and servants. The completely puzzled Arseno, still thinking that it is Ardenia's note, believes that she has learned of his earlier pursuit of Celia and seeks revenge in this manner. In desperation he takes the paper and continues:

ARSENO. "Finally, upon my promise (of marriage)
she gave me what women call
their honor, and what we poets
are accustomed to call 'flower.'"
Celia, I have not possessed you.
This refers to someone else.

CELIA.   If you praise yourself so without,
what would you do if you had?

ARSENO. "Having enjoyed her
I recognized the difference
between uncertain desire
and assured possession.
I became bored and after a few days
I left her, tricked and a fool."
Celia, I have not abandoned you.

CELIA.   You write what you intend to do.

ARSENO. "And to live secure from

> her pursuing and catching me
> I have changed my own name."
> Celia, have I changed my name?
>
> CELIA. In my house you are Arseno.
> I do not know whether you have
> changed it away from my house.
>
> ARSENO. "And he who before was Persio . . ."
>
> CELIA. (Good Heavens!)
>
> ARSENO. Well, what Persio is this,
> that you change color? (vv. 465 et seq.)

Another scene of humor and suspense is the bewilderment of Arseno, the rage of Justino (Ardenia's father), the smug self-satisfaction of Persio, and the reaction of Ardenia when Arseno appears as the "brother" unaware that Persio has already beaten him to the punch. Later in the play, when confusion is at its height, Justino, determined to find out what it is all about, collars Tristán, Persio's servant, and begins to question him. Tristán, believing that Justino knows a good deal more than he really does, and unwilling to take the blame for his master's guilt, blurts out the entire scheme, to the astonishment and consternation of the old man, who admits (v. 2185), "I am finding out more than I expected" (más descubro que pensaba).

The characters are as curious a lot as ever were gathered together in one play. There is hardly a sympathetic or admirable one among them; Ardenia, Celia, Arseno, and Persio are schemers, the father, Justino, is gullible and credulous just at times when he should be the opposite, and the servants are cheaper copies of their masters. Alberto Lista[25] thought the plot ingenious, the versification admirable, and the interest lively, but condemned the characters. On the whole, critics either ignore the play or give it faint praise. Yet, with certain minor reservations, it is a good comedy, in the real sense of the word, unprofound, involved as to plot, entertaining, with rapid action and sparkling dialogue. In the hands of expert actors, it could be amusing theater today.[26]

CHAPTER 3

Comedias *of the* Segunda Parte
(Second Volume)

I   Los empeños de un engaño
(The Entanglements of a Deception)

THE plot of this, another play of intrigue, develops from a
bumbling servant's well-meaning efforts to advance the affairs of his master, an idea that seems to be original with
Alarcón.[1] Castro Leal (p. 120) gives the date as 1615–1618?,
Fernández-Guerra (p. 317) as 1620, and Bruerton, 1621–1625, a
more likely date, since it was not included in the first volume originally ready for publication sometime before January, 1622. The
scene is the Madrid contemporary with the author, and along
with the coincidences, jealousies, schemes, and other ingredients
common to the *comedia,* Alarcón includes a favored one of his
own: the efforts of one woman to thwart the love affair of another.

Leonor lives with her brother, Sancho. Downstairs in the same
house dwell Teodora and her brother, Juan. The plan is for each
man to marry the sister of the other. This uncomplicated and
neatly-laid arrangement is disrupted by the appearance of Don
Diego who is in love with Teodora, but whom Leonor believes to
be in love with her. She has Campana, Diego's servant, summoned
to the house and demands an explanation as to why his master is
appearing there and thus threatening her "honor." Campana does
not wish to reveal that Diego is there because of Teodora and,
therefore, concocts the story that Diego really loves Leonor, but,
to protect *her* honor, pretends to be interested in Teodora. This
engaño, or deception, requires others and after numerous misunderstandings, a challenge, a duel, a threatened murder, even a
leap from a balcony, the situation ends by Diego's marriage to
Teodora, and Leonora's accepting Juan.

Castro Leal (p. 121) thinks that the involved intrigue weighs heavily on the work, but another critic has high praise for "a complicated and agreeable plot, full of interesting incidents, which holds the curiosity of the spectators to the denouement," which "is natural, born of the action itself, and completely satisfies the reader."[2] It is, in fact, a well-wrought comedy, with some unusual details. Alarcón often introduces a variation of the conventional ending; in this case, Leonor rejects a solicitous marquis (and the better choice) merely because he helped Teodora and Diego. He also has Campana marry the servant of Leonor instead of that of his master's wife. There is excellent characterization in the frustrated Diego, the well-intentioned Campana, and the two ladies who are successively friends, rivals, and enemies.

II El dueño de las estrellas (Master of the Stars)

This is the first of a series of five plays in which Alarcón has based his plot on a historical, or pseudohistorical, event.[3] Castro Leal (p. 150) believes that Alarcón probably found his source in Plutarch's *Lives*, which had been translated into Spanish as early as 1491. Although admitting that "nothing can be said [about Lycurgus] which is not disputed," including the time in which he lived, Plutarch promises to try to follow the authors who are "least contradicted."[4] The part of his account most closely concerned with the play is this: Lycurgus was the second son, by a second wife, of his father, and became king of Sparta upon the death of his half-brother, only to learn that his sister-in-law was pregnant. In spite of her suggestion that they destroy the child, marry, and rule together, Lycurgus had the baby proclaimed king upon its birth and himself guardian. Envy and discord caused him to leave Sparta and to go to Crete, among other places. Recalled to Sparta by the citizens, he instituted a number of laws and customs, most of which were designed to strengthen the state. Pleased with his efforts and wishing to make them permanent, he had the citizens sign a solemn oath to make no change in the laws until his return, and then departed for Delphi. There the oracle told him that his laws were good and that they would remain in force as long as he did not return to Sparta, because of the sacred oath made by the citizens. To ensure their perpetuity, Lycurgus starved himself rather than return. According to one version, he ended his days in Crete, where, except for the first scene, Alarcón places the action of his play, which follows the self-imposed exile of Lycurgus, generally assigned to the ninth century B.C., but he has made no effort to recreate the locale or spirit of the times. Bruerton has suggested 1620?–1623? as the date of its composition.

As the play begins, Licurgo (Lycurgus) is living incognito, under the name of Lacón, in a Cretan village. The Delphic oracle tells the King of Crete to seek the "fortunate tree of Licurgo" for his country's ills, which his counselor, Severo, interprets to mean that he should seek out the famous Licurgo and obtain his aid in governing Crete; the tree is the olive, symbol of peace. Licurgo is discovered through a ruse, comes to the court, and eventually marries Severo's daughter, Diana. But the King desires her and when Licurgo comes upon them together in his house, he slays himself because of his dishonor and to defeat another oracular prophecy, which had predicted that he would either kill a king or be killed by one. Hence the title, although from the theme a more accurate one would be "Thwarter of the Stars' Prediction," since he does not really master the stars at all.

The play is not one of Alarcón's best efforts. Castro Leal (p. 154) calls it "a cold work, without inspiration" and it is hardly more than that, although there is something to be said for the manner in which Alarcón has taken the account of Plutarch and made it conform to the requirements of the *comedia*. Nor is the ending a satisfying one. Not only does Licurgo kill himself, but the King immediately offers to marry Diana (and she accepts) as the least he can do for being instrumental in her husband's death. Alarcón's introduction of suicide as a solution has been noted as daring, but he was dealing with a legendary, perhaps historical, episode and a pagan society so that he was neither original nor in conflict with the Christian condemnation of self-destruction.

The characters are very disappointing. Licurgo in his best moments is an example of rectitude, wisdom, and self-sacrifice, as befits a Spartan statesman, but this is inconsistent with the characteristics of the seventeenth-century *galán* with whom he is confused: amorous, loyal to an unworthy sovereign, and insistent upon avenging a personal insult. The King is a sorry picture of lust, a vice which overcomes even a desire to rule wisely. Diana's firmness in first resisting the King's advances evaporates as the play progresses. Some, like Teón, who runs off with another man's wife, slaps Licurgo, and is murdered for his rashness, and Marcela, who is ready to compromise her cousin's honor, are far from admirable.

Interesting, although extraneous to the plot, are the six "laws" which Licurgo offers (Act III) to the King of Crete. Although the "laws" seem to be Alarcón's, the idea was suggested by the appearance in 1618 (Madrid) of *Proverbios morales y consejos cristianos* (*Moral Proverbs and Christian Counsel*) by Cristóbal Pérez de Herrera, to which Alarcón had dedicated two *quintillas,* and at the end of which appear "fourteen proposals which seem to be very important for the well-being and peace of these kingdoms" (*catorce proposiciones que aparecen ser muy importantes para el bien y descanso de estos reinos*). Pérez offers ideas which he thinks will improve the economic life of the country and then elaborates on how his suggestions could be carried out. Similarly, Alarcón proposes a "law" (in prose) and then explains its purpose and its implementation (but in verse). They propose to eliminate idleness among the *plebeyos* (common people), to force a sort of draft law on all members of the nobility, to provide for a widow, to grant the rights and privileges of the native Spaniard to foreigners who take up residence in Spain, to pay officers of justice according to need rather than a fixed income, and to force a criminal to continue residing at the scene of his crime so that the neighbors may keep an eye on him.

III　La amistad castigada (Friendship Punished)

Bruerton suggests 1621 as the date of this play, and Castro Leal (p. 154) a year or so earlier, or about the same time as that of *Master of the Stars,* to which it has some similarities. For his subject, Alarcón turned once more to Plutarch, this time for the history of Dionysius II, tyrant of Syracuse, who ruled Sicily from 367 to 356 B.C., and again from 347 to 343. He was the eldest son of his father by one of two wives that he had at the time. Dion, brother of the other wife, both because of this relationship and his own worth, achieved a high place in the esteem of the elder Dionysius. He seems to have been intellectually endowed, a philosopher, and a friend of Plato. By marrying Arete, who was his own niece as well as a half-sister of Dionysius the younger, he became both uncle and brother-in-law to the future tyrant. Although his real opinion of his nephew was not a very high one,

Dion took an interest in him and sought to make him a philosopher-king, but without success. After a period of struggle between uncle and nephew, Dion finally triumphed, but his efforts to restore order were futile and he was slain in 343 B.C. by a conspirator. Alarcón retains the two historical characters, Dionysius II and Dion, whom he makes brothers-in-law. He also incorporates the exile of the king, but, as in *Master of the Stars,* changes the motive from that of statesmanship to one of honor, and he alters another situation by having Dionisio in love with his own niece (Aurora, the daughter of Dion). The play's ending, the forced exile of Dionisio by Dion, is but one incident in Plutarch: At a point early in the struggle for power, Dion requested Dionysius to give up his sovereignty and he, Dion, "would himself procure immunity for him and any other reasonable privilege that was in his power, mindful of the close relationship between them." [5]

Dionisio, King of Sicily, although betrothed to another, desires Aurora for his pleasure. She already has two suitors, one of whom had earlier compromised another lady, Diana. A fourth *galán* is Filipo, the King's favorite, who falls in love with Aurora while on a visit to advance the King's affair. His passion overcomes his loyalty as a favorite and he informs Dion of Dionisio's plot to seduce Aurora during Dion's absence. The sudden appearance of her father saves Aurora and his own honor. Since Dion has put the King on his throne, he reserves the right to remove him, and forces him into exile. He also banishes Filipo, who had hoped to marry Aurora, with the reason that if he could betray one king he would also betray another. On the other hand he rewards Turpín, an old, venal servant, who had permitted the King to enter the house, because he obeyed his king even though it meant a risk to Dion's honor.

The play is too contrived to be effective. As Castro Leal (p. 155) points out, "the *comedia* sets forth, in an imperfect way, a purely ideological problem. Does friendship justify an act of disloyalty to the king?" Yet, he continues, Alarcón does not answer this question, because Filipo does not represent real friendship. He acts continually according to his self-interest. He is in love with Aurora and he betrays his king, not because of his concern with the king's misdeeds, nor because he admires Dion or approves of him, but solely because he believes that his actions will win Aurora for himself. Even Fernández-Guerra (p. 277) thought

that the play lacked interest, because "the characters which
[Alarcón] presents are defective and the moral solutions or appli-
cations are unjust and contradictory." The characters are indeed
defective. The King's preoccupation with his passion makes him
unworthy of his trust. Dion does not have the force or the motivation that marked the historical model. Filipo is weak and disloyal.
Aurora, clever enough, shows a curious contrariness in siding with
the King against her father, just because he is the king, moments
after Dionisio has tried to force himself upon her. There is no real
gracioso, the closest being the servant Turpín. His being rewarded for "obeying" the command of the King to admit him to
Dion's house is illogical since his real reason for opening the door
was the handsome bribe that he was given. One good scene (Act
I) is the exchange between Filipo and Aurora in which the latter
tries her best to get her hesitant suitor to declare himself and
finally succeeds.

IV   La manganilla de Melilla (The Stratagem at Melilla)

Melilla is a Spanish military enclave on the northern coast of
Africa, within, but not part of the territory of Morocco. Captured
by the Spaniards from the Arabs in 1496, it was governed during
the years 1561 to 1568 by Pedro Venegas de Córdoba. In 1563, "a
great number of Moors, seduced and deceived by the promises of
a fanatic *alfaquí* to make them masters of the fortress of Melilla
by beguiling the Christians who were defending it, attack it with
great resolution. Don Pedro Venegas, its governor, allows them to
enter, and [his] troops who were in ambush throw themselves
upon them and cause a cruel slaughter. The *alfaquí* is wounded,
but he saves himself by fleeing and a short time later he persuades
[his men] again to attack the fortress, promising them greater
success. Twenty-five thousand men attack it and they are completely routed." [6] Don Pedro died in Madrid in 1600, the year
Alarcón first came to Spain.[7] For this reason, perhaps, Castro Leal
(p. 88) assigns to the play the dates 1602 to 1608?, but it seems
unlikely that the death of Don Pedro in Madrid would have made
that much impression on a twenty-year-old student at Salamanca,
just arrived from Mexico. Bruerton suggests the dates 1618? to
1623. The play perhaps was not ready in time for inclusion in the
first volume of his *comedias*, prepared in early 1622 at the latest,
and this implies a later date. As Castro Leal (p. 88) suggests,

there may have been available to Alarcón an oral tradition or a *romance* (ballad) alluding to and even exaggerating the affair.

The focus of the play is the stratagem of Pedro Vanegas. To it are added the love of the captive Moorish maiden, Alima, for Pedro, the perfidious conduct of Pimienta, another of Alarcón's more disagreeable characters, the efforts of the Moor, Azén, to get back Alima, to whom he was once promised, and the activities of the mysterious Moor and magician, Amet. It is the last who advises that the Moors enter Melilla unarmed and he will aid in its capture, but they disobey him and secretly carry weapons. When Vanegas learns of the plot, allows them to enter, and surrounds them all, they blame Amet, who tells them that they failed because of their disobedience. Then he disappears and the question is asked as to who he was. An angel? The episode of the attack, ambush, and defeat is a dramatic one and a good play might have been composed, but Alarcón failed to meet the challenge. Instead it is a rather tawdry attempt to appeal to the public taste; there are magical tricks and a repulsive scene which reflects the anti-Semitic attitude of the time.

Castro Leal (p. 91) thought the construction "able," but that Alarcón missed the opportunity of presenting an epic treatment. Although Fernández-Guerra (p. 218) deplores the irrelevant episodes, he thought that the play had as its argument and purpose "the moral end of celebrating the dominion of the Christian faith," but Valbuena Prat[8] comments that "in spite of the protestation of the Christian faith by Alima, the fervent feeling of Catholicism is far from having the fervid accents of Calderón's *El príncipe constante* (*The Constant Prince*) or even of *Los baños de Argel* (*The Prisons of Algiers*) by Cervantes." In fact, the practice of Christianity becomes an unintentional farce. Alima, for example, after a long argument with Vanegas, in which she convinces him that she wants to become a Christian, turns on her pursuer, Azén, and declares that because she hates him so, she will kill him—and does. Again, although Vanegas is hesitant about accepting Alima as a Christian because he suspects that her desire to be one is dictated only by her eagerness to escape Azén, he will later stand before the captured Moors, raise an image of Christ and say:

Vile Moors!
This is the image of Christ.

He alone is the true God.
Those who accept His law
will be free;
the rest, if they do not yield
as captives, will die.

> (¡ *Moros viles,*
> *la imagen de Cristo es ésta!*
> *Él solo es Dios verdadero:*
> *los que a su ley se conviertan*
> *de vosotros, serán libres;*
> *los demás, si no se entregan*
> *por cautivos, morirán!*) (vv. 2795–2801)

As one commentator remarks: "Where is the 'voluntary consent' (*voluntario movimiento*) that he had earlier demanded of Alima?" [9] Notwithstanding its mellifluous title and the extravagant praise of one critic,[10] the play must be adjudged one of the weakest of Alarcón's dramatic efforts.

V   La verdad sospechosa (The Truth Suspect)

In sharp contrast to *The Stratagem at Melilla* is the play that follows it in the edition of 1634. Not only is *The Truth Suspect* Alarcón's best and most famous work, but in construction and in universal and lasting appeal it may very well be the finest play to issue from any pen of the *Siglo de Oro*. It proves rather conclusively that Alarcón's forte lay in drama contemporary with his period, set in Madrid or other places with which he was familar, and developed from a deception or misunderstanding; he was much less successful in historical or foreign subjects. The date of its composition is given as 1619 or 1620; certainly it was written prior to March 31, 1621, the day of the death of Felipe III, to whom Alarcón alludes in the play as still living. The scene is Madrid of the same period.

Efforts have been made to find a source for the play, as if one were needed. John Brooks has pointed out similarities between it and the *Adelphoe* of Terence. Arthur L. Owen and Elisa Pérez believe that it has elements of the *Andria* of the same Roman playwright; Richard Tyler has suggested as a possible influence *ejemplo* 284 of *El libro de los exemplos por A. B. C.* (*The Book of Examples Alphabetically Arranged*) by Clemente Sánchez de

Vercial (d. 1426), and Miriam V. Melvin notes the 26th *ejemplo* of Juan Manuel (d. *ca.* 1348) in his *El conde Lucanor.*[11] Alarcón was acquainted with Terence; he refers to him by name and as a kindred spirit in *Todo es ventura* (*Everything Is Chance*) (v. 797), remarking that Romans whistled derisively at *his* plays too, but his influence on Alarcón's plays has been greatly overrated. He might, as well, have known of the other sources suggested, but it was not necessary to go to them for the plot, which is really one more version of the fable of the boy who cried "wolf."

Not infrequently during this era, a play was inspired by, and constructed around, a proverb, and there was one made to order for Alarcón: "In the mouth of a liar, the truth is always questionable" (*En boca mentirosa, la verdad siempre es dudosa*). Another version was "the only gain a liar gets is that no one believes him when he speaks the truth" (*El mentiroso no gana más de que no le crean cuando dice verdad*); still another, "the liar is not believed when he tells the truth" (*El mentiroso no es creído cuando dice verdad*), and a final one, "he who is considered a liar, even if he tells the truth, is not believed" (*El que por mentiroso es tenido, aunque diga verdad, no es creído*).[12] The difficulties that arise from the first deception have been stated by the maid, Inés, in *The Unlucky Feigner,* by Don Juan in *The Resembler of Himself,* and by Don Diego in *The Entanglement of a Deception.*[13]

A young man, Don García, with a vivid imagination, to whom making an impression, building ego, is more important than telling the truth, falls in love with a girl whose name is not what he thinks it is, an error that is compounded by his penchant for invention and exaggeration. To lie or not to keep one's word was one of the worst lapses of a man of honor and Don Beltrán, his father, proposes as a solution to this threat to the family name his getting married as soon as possible, before the boy's fault may become known. The father's choice of a wife for his son is the very girl of whom García has become enamored, but because of the confusion of names, García invents a number of fabrications in order to avoid the marriage, learning only too late that he has lied himself out of a marriage with the girl he loves.

Fernández-Guerra (p. 306) thought the play "highly moral and full of life through its characters taken from nature itself and the capital of Felipe III portrayed by seizing the truthful brush of Velázquez; it reflects the feeling of every century and every nation, to the point that, if the characters were to change costumes, any epoch and any society would esteem as its own this picture." Arthur L. Owen (*op. cit.*, p. xx) writes that "at times, as in . . . *The Truth Suspect* (mendacity), . . . he devotes the whole of the argument of a play to assailing a vice or exalting a virtue." Many others have stressed the "moral" of the play, but Castro Leal (pp. 135–36) makes a more valued judgment:

The Truth Suspect is not an invective against liars. It is a *comedia* of joy which shows a certain youthful pleasure in life. It corresponds to that type of work which is represented, at its highest level, by Shakespeare's *Comedy of Errors* and Wilde's *The Importance of Being Earnest.* It is a comedy which rests on situations mentally and artificially constructed, which lives from its own exultation and in which the characters are sketched perspicaciously and excellently, but also with a freedom of outline that, without reducing their vitality, makes them docile playthings of a happy mood, a youthful and joyful world. He who does not keep this in mind will lose the best part of the comedy. . . . Don García is finally punished not because of having lied, but simply because he confused Jacinta with Lucrecia. The comedy has no didactic purpose and we should be grateful to Alarcón that in it he has not rounded off those edges upon which those who seek to show that *The Truth Suspect* is the work of a moralist always stumble.

Castro Leal considers the ending rather unconvincing to the audience since, although necessary to the plot, it comes about not from the defect in García's character, but from mistaken identity even though García's innocent and original error was continued and compounded by his telling tall tales. It is a magnificent comedy in spite of a few implausible devices for prolonging the confusion and presents Alarcón at his best in carefully working out a plot, introducing the elements of coincidence, mistaken identity, and chance so as to keep the play moving and the interest at a high point at all times.

The Truth Suspect has been called the best comedy of character produced in the Classic period,[14] and Don García, if not quite so famous as his literary contemporary, Don Juan, is as well defined. In spite of his "vice," he is an ingratiating character, "magnanimous, valiant, wise, clever, liberal and compassionate, if impulsive and impatient," according to his tutor (vv. 141–44). García him-

self explains his propensity for fabricating as a desire to make an
impression:

> To be famous is a great thing;
> whatever the means.
> Let me be named everywhere,
> let them even gossip about me.

> (*Ser famoso es gran cosa;*
> *el medio cual fuere sea.*
> *Nómbrenme a mí en todas partes*
> *y murmúrenme siquiera.*) (vv. 861–64)

Besides such an untruth as claiming that he is a wealthy *indiano*
(a Spaniard recently returned from the New World), he contrib-
utes a lengthy invention to each act, the most important of which
is that of Act II: To avoid marriage to his father's choice, García,
on the spur of the moment, gives an imaginary account of how he
was forced to marry a lady in Salamanca after having been caught
with her in a compromising situation. It is a comedy in miniature,
embellished with a vivid description of fighting, fainting, pistol
shooting, and a near escape from death. So artful is the story that
his father is completely taken in, even though he knows his son as
a liar and has just denounced lying as being the only vice from
which there is no compensatory pleasure or profit.

Another character of interest is the father, Beltrán, well presented in the position of an anxious and indulgent parent, grieving
over the death of an older favorite and promising son, and having
to cope with what to him is the dishonorable conduct of his second son. His distress at learning that García has small regard for
the truth is understandable, but his solution, immediate marriage,
is, to say the least, illogical. Like García, he has one defect in an
otherwise exemplary character: his greater concern for the family
name than for his son's welfare. Tristán, the servant, or as Beltrán
puts it, "not a servant . . . but adviser and friend" (vv. 17–18), is
dignified, intelligent, somewhat learned, and helpful. He is amusing, but in a dignified way. Even his comparison of women, from
those of impeccable conduct to prostitutes, with heavenly bodies,
is done with taste.[15] The second *galán*, Don Juan, is a jealous, self-
centered lover, seemingly more interested in his own advance-

ment than in his lady, Jacinta, but annoyed when he thinks she is being courted by someone else. The two ladies, Jacinta and Lucrecia, remain throughout the play rather shadowy figures. Neither one has much to do with determining the action; rather they are objects of a misunderstanding which they are unable to resolve. In fact, they are so undistinguished and undistinguishable that it does not really matter which one García marries, as Corneille was later to show in his version of the play.

The Truth Suspect has had a diffusion second only to El burlador de Sevilla (The Trickster of Sevilla), attributed to Tirso de Molina, but in a different way and for different reasons. Whereas it is the sensual aspect of the character of Don Juan that has been adopted and adapted in other literatures, it is the theme of The Truth Suspect that has been imitated. Pierre Corneille, the French playwright who had earlier adapted a Spanish play, was so impressed by El mentiroso (The Liar) that (in 1642 or 1643) he wrote a version for the French classic theater "partly translated and partly imitated." [16] The plot seemed to him so clever, so well shaped, he adds, that he would have given two of his best plays had it been of his own invention.[17]

Besides composing his work in the neoclassic manner, Corneille made a number of other changes, the most radical being that of having Dorante (García) suspect his error and note the attractions of Lucrèce (Lucrecia) so that when he is finally required to marry her, the marriage will appear less forced and thus "more to the taste of our audience." One editor of Le Menteur thinks the "corrections," in general, "happy," and that the French comedy is better constructed, more temperate, of a tauter composition and, "so far as one can judge," of a simpler, more direct, and firm style.[18] Those well acquainted with the Spanish original, however, will probably prefer its varied versification, lighter tone, more rapid action, and more interesting characterization.

Having seen a performance of Corneille's play, the Italian dramatist, Carlo Goldoni, made (in 1750) a version of his own, Il Bugiardo (The Liar). In this delightful comedy, written in prose, the protagonist is completely a liar and deceiver. After misleading two ladies purposely, he is forced to marry a third whom he had earlier seduced. Alarcón's masterpiece returned to Madrid in 1793 in the disguise of a Spanish translation of Goldoni's play. Meanwhile (1764) an English version, The Lyar, also based on Corneille's, was prepared by Samuel Foote. In prose, it is even more of a farce than Goldoni's and the liar gets his deserts when one of the ladies, more perspicacious than her predecessors, persuades someone to impersonate the supposed wife.[19] There are many other versions, too numerous to be mentioned here, all stemming from that of Corneille,[20] so that he must be credited with the diffusion of the theme, but even though imitation may be the sincerest form of flattery, none can compare with the masterpiece of Alarcón, which started it all.[21]

VI   Ganar amigos (How to Win Friends)

The concept of *la amistad* (friendship) in the Spanish *comedia* ranks with loyalty to one's lord, honor, and love among the more important motivations of its characters. But the concept is limited and peculiar—one that is rather the idea of obligation or gratitude than affection or intimacy. A man of honor defends and befriends another man (of his own station) in difficulty or promises to do so, a promise that the code required be kept. In turn, the recipient is grateful and under obligation to his benefactor. On this basis, a "friendship" is struck, and can be formed even between strangers. Men thus obligated could be of help in future difficulties. The theme is used in a number of plays including this one of Alarcón, which in some editions bears the title *Lo que mucho vale, mucho cuesta, en ganar amigos* (*What Is Worth Much Costs Much in Winning Friends*). It introduces one historical character, King Pedro of Castile, known both as "the Cruel" and as "the Just," who ruled from 1350 to 1369. This hot-tempered but energetic monarch, who did many enemies to death, is perhaps more frequently portrayed in the *comedia* than any other Spanish ruler, sometimes, as in this play, as the dispenser of justice, the one who resolves the difficulties and brings the play to an end. The action, then, is during his reign, and in Sevilla, but it has no other historical basis.

The idea for the plot may have been suggested by a proverb emphasizing the value of friendship, such as "winning friends is to lend money at interest and to sow in irrigated land" (*Ganar amigos es dar dinero a logro, y sembrar en regadío*).[22] Miss Melvin cites the 18th *ejemplo* of Juan Manuel in connection with *Ganar amigos,*[23] in which a certain Meléndez de Valdés is condemned to death through the false accusations of his enemies, but is saved when, on the way to his execution, he falls from his horse and breaks a leg, thus allowing time for the king to learn the truth and to pardon him. According to Castro Leal (p. 145), the *comedia* was written in 1617–1618?, but Bruerton dates it 1620?–1622.[24]

The play is replete with coincidence, *escondites* (hiding places), duels, deceptions, and trysts. The Marquis Fadrique offers his protection to a stranger (Fernando) in trouble, who, it develops, has not only murdered the brother of the marquis in a duel, but has been making advances to Flor, the object of his affections. At Flor's request, Fernando has sworn to keep secret his interest in her, and the marquis, having committed himself to Fernando's protection is bound to continue it. Interwoven with the main plot are the affair between another *galán and dama,* Diego and Doña Ana, and the efforts of the king to have a courtier murdered because of an indiscretion in the palace. The conflict between human desires and the demands of the code of honor leads Fadrique to prison and the shadow of the block, but on the way he has obligated three men by favors so that in the end, even though they have been individually responsible for the plight of the marquis, they offer to die in his stead. The king overhears this demonstration of "friendship" and is so impressed that he accepts their explanations and pardons all.[25]

In spite of the "patness" of the events, the questionable taste of a seduction episode, and the contrived means of "winning friends," this is a splendidly constructed play. Critics are lavish in their praise of it,[26] and it has received a number of translations into French, German, and Italian. Whatever moderns may think of the code of honor, it formed the *modus operandi* of his play and Alarcón has introduced the various facets of this intricate and refined code in a logical and persuasive manner. The interplay of love, loyalty, gratitude, honor, with the strand of intrigue weaving in and out is ingenious, and clearly presents the limits that the inborn and inbred sense of honor placed on personal ambition and desire. Fernando can pester Flor, Diego can seduce Ana, Pedro de Luna can violate the palace code, and the king can summarily order a man's execution, but when the chips are down, the code of honor, which was designed to bring out the noblest in a man, triumphs, and all is resolved.

The male characters are well presented as personalities:

Fadrique is always the upright man; he can accept his brother's death because it occurred in a fair fight, but he hesitates to murder a man when he believes that the king has acted rashly. Fernando is something of a nuisance as he annoys Flor, but he is willing even to die to protect her name and his promise of secrecy. Don Diego, frantic over the possible stain on his family's honor through the indiscretions of Flor, his sister, is not above scheming to bribe his way into another lady's house in order to seduce her, thus dishonoring both her and her family. The ladies, like many in the later dramas and quite unlike those in some of the earlier ones, are less distinctive.

VII   El Anticristo (The Antichrist)

Although *The Stratagem at Melilla* has strong religious overtones, *The Antichrist* is Alarcón's only intentional essay into the genre of religious drama, and it reveals, in Castro Leal's understatement, "his scant sympathy for the genre [and] makes one think that it was written under circumstances that were never again to appear in his life." And just as well, for it ranks with *The Stratagem at Melilla* as his least happy effort.

The Antichrist was almost certainly written in 1623, for on December 14 of this year it received its first performance under circumstances which can be described as unusual (*supra*, p. 30). Castro Leal (pp. 117–19) poses an interesting hypothesis to the effect that it was begun in the years 1606–1608, when Alarcón was in Sevilla, and was inspired by "interesting and repeated conversations with the Father Diego Ruiz de Montoya, eminent theologian and his relative," and that he took it up again in 1615 to 1618. He bases this conjecture on his belief that "the spirit of religious conviction and of sincere acceptance of the theme, which dominates the first two acts, disappears almost completely in the third." The lack of any evidence that Alarcón wrote plays prior to his return to Spain and settling in Madrid has already been stressed. The change of direction which the play takes, in this case from a serious work to a rather preposterous one, is not unique. Although not in the same way or even to the same extent, we find a shift in direction in *The Stratagem at Melilla* and shall see it again in *Los pechos privilegiados* (*Privileged Breasts*).

Alarcón drew his inspiration from the writings of Sts. Matthew, Mark, Luke, and Paul, the Apocalypse of St. John, and the Book of Daniel, as well as the *Tratado del juicio final y universal* (*Treatise of the Final and Universal Judgment*) by Nicolás Díaz, which he cites in the play and which appeared in 1588. Padre Díaz was at one time a professor at the University of Salamanca.[27] The word "antichrist" is first used by St. John in his first epistle, Chapter II, verse 18, but the ideas embodied in an antichrist go back into Jewish eschatology and changed not only during the beginning of the Christian era, but continually through the Middle Ages to the time of Alarcón. His interpretation represents the theological belief prevailing in the sixteenth and seventeenth centuries, based partly on an apparently good acquaintance with the Bible and partly on theological and popular treatises of his own day.[28]

The plot is a gruesome one: A false Elijah appears ("Behold I will send you Elijah the prophet, before the coming of the great and dreadful day of the Lord," [Malachi, IV, 5]) and tells his companions that he has seen a great vision, taken from Daniel (VII, 13) and the Apocalypse (XII, 5) in which the promised Messiah is to reappear, showing them the palm of his hand with the mark P on it.[29] He and his companions then seek out this "Messiah," in order to serve him. Since the Antichrist is the child of incest as was his mother, an indecent contrast with the immaculate conception of Christ and His Mother, the Antichrist decides to be the opposite of Christ in every way and becomes the personification of the utmost wickedness. He slays his mother and attempts to possess Sofía, but since she, almost alone, recognizes him as false and denounces him, he eventually orders her beheaded.[30] He declares himself King of Babilonia, assumes the name of the god Maozín and encourages his cult, and orders the death of one of his followers when he turns against him. Some Biblical prophecies are fulfilled,[31] but finally his followers desert him, his power crumbles, and, with the false Elijah, he is sent to Hell by an angel of the Lord.

The play, intended to be a serious work, is almost a caricature. There are several scenes of magic in which someone is rising or descending in the air by means of a *tramoya* (stage machinery), allegorical scenes in which Libya, Ethiopia, and Egypt appear as persons, some incredibly long speeches, debates, quotations from the work of Nicolás Díaz, a pinch of an honor theme in the efforts of Sofía to keep her virtue in spite of the Antichrist, and liberal doses of Christian doctrine and biblical references. There is a *gracioso*, Balán, an independent personage in that he is not the servant of anyone,[32] but he has the traits (credulity, timidity, lack of loyalty) of a *gracioso*, and his experiences serve as digression and diversion, if not edification.

The work has not been favored by the critics. Castro Leal (pp. 119–20) thought that the scenic presentation was beyond the power of Alarcón. Valbuena Prat damns it as "one of the worst *comedias de santos* [*comedias* about saints] of our entire theater, a true 'flop,' in which the apocalyptic drama is changed into a parody . . ." In another place he exclaims: "What an absurd accumulation of horrors, of incest and parricides, in order to make the protagonist odious; what an abuse of flights, apparitions, and superficial miracle-making (*milagrería*)! A work that sought to have a thrust and which demonstrated an absolute ineptitude, . . . demonstrates [also] an almost negative attitude toward the religious feeling of the epoch. Of *El Anticristo*, scarcely anything is saved beyond the jokes of the *gracioso*." [33] Even these are in rather poor taste. Menéndez y Pelayo thought that it is in some points "magnificent and grandiloquent," but admitted its imperfection.[34]

VIII El tejedor de Segovia (The Weaver of Segovia)

Although usually known as the *segunda parte* (second part) of a two-play series with this title, Alarcón wrote only this "part." The source of its subject has not been determined. Fernández-Guerra (pp. 353–54) attributes its composition to a revulsion against the disgrace of the Dukes of Osuna and Uceda and the execution of Rodrigo Calderón, men who had risen high in power, wealth, and influence during the reign of Felipe III, but who fell upon evil days:

He remembers the skillful means of escape which the prisoners in the prison of Sevilla put into effect and how, as if by magic, they knew how to get their freedom and mock the severity of their persecutors. And overcome by a sort of frenzy, Ruiz de Alarcón puts Terence and Plautus aside, forgets Horace and Aristotle, his classical guides, and at the impulse of the feeling which exalts and excites him, he writes *El tejedor de Segovia*.[35]

One would like to think that Alarcón was so moved, but it is much more likely that, as Fernández-Guerra also suggests (p. 354), and Castro Leal with him (p. 166), it was "some common tradition about the strange adventures of a certain Don Fernando Ramírez de Vargas, which likely had come alive in some neglected *romance*" and thus "Don Juan chose to satisfy the vehemence of his imaginings. He put the story back five and a half centuries, taking it to the reign of Don Alfonso [VI], he who won Toledo; but he did not want to bother studying that remote period, convinced, without doubt, that all are alike, and painted his own without changing a tittle." Verses 1798–1827, 1831, and 1990–1991, form a *romance*, or ballad, which is sung and which refers to the exploits of Pedro Alonso and his companions. Although tailored to the plot, something similar may have suggested to Alarcón the idea for his play, which was probably written between 1619 and 1622 as Castro Leal (p. 166) and Bruerton suggest.

It is not until near the end of the play that we learn the details that have brought about the situation with which it opens, but Fernando Ramírez de Vargas has assumed the name of Pedro Alonso, a weaver of Segovia, until such time as he can wreak vengeance for the wrongs that have been done him and his family by his enemies, the Marquis Suero Peláez and his son, Juan. As a result of a scuffle with Juan, Fernando (as Pedro) is cast into prison from which he escapes and with a band of loyal followers hides out in the Guadarrama Mountains to await the day of triumph; here Teodora, his wife, disguised as a man, joins them.[36] In the end, the valiant band of one hundred men turns back an invading Moorish army and rescues the fleeing Spanish King, Alfonso VI, who now has the opportunity to learn of the injustice done Fernando and to permit its being righted. After forcing Juan to marry his (Fernando's) sister whom he had seduced, Fernando marries her, now a "widow," to his vassal, Garcerán; then, exacting a confession of his misdeeds from the marquis, he slays him also.

Alphonse M. Royer believes that this play is "the most violent creation of our Mexican poet; . . . characters, thoughts, countryside, language, everything is rugged and excessive. Vengeance, a feeling so dear to ancient Spain, here is relished in long draughts; since it is founded on a just cause, it rises almost to the height of a virtue and in witnessing its inflexible execution, the spectator feels attracted toward the heroic bandit by a sympathy from which he cannot escape." [37] The play is indeed filled with action, suspense, heroic deeds, and matters of honor.

The major characters are among Alarcón's most forceful. Fernando is aggressive, astute, brave, sensitive to his honor, a good strategist, and loyal to his king. It seems somewhat unworthy of him to rob travelers and villagers, but he does insist on not harming the victims and it is done out of necessity rather than wickedness. Garcerán, too, is a noble, brave, and loyal man, more sensitive to his honor even than to love. The two women are also energetic figures. Teodora is willing to undergo hardships to be with her husband and even hits upon a clever ruse by which she secures Juan's sword in order to save both her husband and herself. Ana, Fernando's sister, remains, in spite of her dishonor, a person of spirit. In one scene, knowing that Garcerán would not marry her if he knew the truth and unwilling to confess her shame, she prefers to pretend that she really loves another in order to discourage his attentions. The iniquitous count, Juan, is but the worst of several characters of the type in Alarcón, a man of noble blood but base instincts. Even his father, in the manner of Don Beltrán in *The Truth Suspect*, has occasion (vv. 575–638) to scold his son for his behavior, reminding him that being a gentleman (*señor*) consists in conduct (*obrar bien*) rather than heredity, strange words from a man who had earlier caused the death of a man through lying, but indicative of the paradox that exists in the code of the *comedia* by which a man can act dishonorably (at least in the modern interpretation of the word) and yet possess a sense of honor.

The play differs in a number of important ways from any other written by Alarcón.[38] There is no real love intrigue. Fernando and Teodora are already married, the only work of Alarcón in which the *galán* is married throughout. The solution to Ana's dishonor is the death of her seducer; other cases of dishonor by seduction are resolved by marriage. It has been classified as a romantic drama, a social drama, and a drama of defiance. The idea of outlawry appealed to the Romantic mind and *The Weaver of Segovia* has that Romantic touch. It received four translations into French during the nineteenth century and may have been the first play of Alarcón to be performed in Mexico (1805–1806).[39] One of the few

plays of the *Siglo de Oro* to survive into eighteenth-century Spain,
it was revived during the Romantic period, for the season of 1834,
at which time it was favorably compared with the French Romantic drama.[40] Some critics have seen in it an influence for Hugo's
Hernani and Schiller's *Die Räuber* (*The Robbers*).[41] Certainly the
protagonist in each play is an outlaw, but in the former, love is a
stronger motive than Hernani's desire to correct a grievance, and
in the second, von Moor's acts as an outlaw are much more hei-
nous than those of Fernando. The rebel against society is not infrequently portrayed in the *comedia* of the era, but *The Weaver
of Segovia* is not a protest drama. Fernando has one purpose—
and that a purely selfish one—which is to put himself beyond the
clutches of an unscrupulous enemy until such time as he can obtain redress for the wrongs done to him. The code of honor did
not allow for recourse to law, but required that the injured man
resolve the matter himself. *Hernani* and *The Robbers* end tragi-
cally, but the finale of *The Weaver of Segovia* is conventional:
Fernando restores the besmirched family honor, demonstrates his
absolute loyalty to the king, and is returned to favor.[42]

An indication of the popularity of the play is the existence of a
Primera parte or "First Part," which dramatizes the events prior to
the second part as recited in Alarcón's play. It is not known when
it was written or first published; the earliest dated edition is that
of Antonio Sanz, 1745. Although most scholars now reject the play
as Alarcón's,[43] there are still some who maintain that it is his.[44] It is
poorly written and weakly constructed. Castro Leal (p. 165) calls
it "a commercial product of the seventeenth century, . . . written
by a poet with a facile pen, . . . with scenes of love and defiance
to entertain the public," unworthy of the fame and fortune that it
has received as a result of being coupled to the authentic *Tejedor.*[45]

IX   La prueba de las promesas (The Test of Promises)

The *Infante,* or Prince, Don Juan Manuel (1282–1348) was a
nephew of Alfonso X, *el sabio,* or "the Learned" (d. 1284), and
shared his uncle's interests in literature. Among his many writings
is a collection of fifty-one "exemplary tales" (*ejemplos*) or charm-
ingly retold versions of apologues or fables, in each of which a
Count Lucanor presents a personal problem to his advisor, Pa-
tronio, who in turn replies by means of an example or illustration.

The eleventh tale is about a dean of the cathedral of Santiago who desired to learn the art of black magic, related to answer the query of the count as to whether he should continue to aid a man who under some pretext or another continually refuses to return a favor. Having heard of the prowess of Don Illán in his art, the dean traveled to Toledo to persuade the magician to give him lessons:

But Don Illán told him that he was a dean and a man of position within the Church and that he could still rise much and that men who rise high when they have achieved what they seek, forget very quickly what others have done for them; because of which he [Don Illán] was afraid that when he had learned what he wanted he would no longer be grateful to him nor would he want to do for him what he now was promising.

The dean assured him that he might have any post he wished; he had only to ask. Thereupon, Don Illán called a servant to prepare some partridges for supper but not to begin roasting them until she was told, and the dean and his teacher descended to the latter's study. No sooner had the lessons begun than messages came announcing the illness and death of the dean's uncle, an archbishop, and his own elevation to the archbishopric. As predicted, the ex-dean continued to rise in the hierarchy until at last he was elected pope, but he never fulfilled his promise to give the most recently vacated post to Don Illán's son. When the new pope was reminded of it, he became annoyed, and threatened to put Don Illán in prison if he bothered him again, "since he knew that he was a heretic and a wizard." Refused food for the return journey as well, Don Illán confessed that he would, therefore, have to eat the partridges which he had ordered for that night. He summoned the servant, which broke the spell, and the astonished "pope" found himself still a dean in the study of Don Illán, acutely embarrassed that the charges of the worthlessness of his promises should have been so manifestly proven.

Of the story, Alarcón retained only the character of Don Illán, the illusion of the passing of time, and the theme of the nonfulfillment of promises. Don Illán, the necromancer, is now Don Illán de Toledo, head of a house which for years has been feuding with that of Don Enrique de Vargas. The partridges are replaced by a fine horse and Don Illán is to be advised when he is saddled so as to show him off. The love affair, absent in the tale but essential to the *comedia*, is introduced in the person of Doña Blanca, Don Illán's daughter. Her father wants her to marry Enrique and bring an end to the feud, but she prefers Juan. To be close to her, Juan persuades Don Illán to give him lessons in black magic. Juan rises in the social scale until he is a marquis and president of the Council of Castile, but he continues to excuse himself from keeping his promise to Don Illán. He even refuses to marry Blanca because she is now his social inferior, but he still desires her for his pleasure. When, like the "pope," he denounces Don Illán, the servant appears to announce that the horse is now ready. The spell is broken, Juan is humiliated, and Blanca, disillusioned in him, accepts Enrique. Alarcón limits the scene of action to Toledo and Madrid (although only by illusion since the characters are supposed never to have left the study), and brings the time of the events to his own.

This is one of Alarcón's most ingenious compositions, superbly wrought. The plot is uncomplicated and direct, and except for one digression in the nature of a job-seeking scene, the action is unified. There are several amusing and diverting scenes in which the servants take part, and Alarcón has also given us some interesting characterizations: Lucía, Blanca's wily maid, who, although committed to the cause of Enrique, is more impressed by the wealth and power of Juan; Tristán, Juan's servant, who is clever and a schemer and even insists on being addressed as "don" when his master's fortunes improve; Illán, upright and astute (except in his misguided confidence in his daughter's maid); Juan, the untrustworthy suitor of Blanca, who, unlike García of *The Truth Suspect*, gets no lady at all as a lesson for his misconduct; Enrique, also a suitor of Blanca, a good portrayal of frustration, despair, and ineffectiveness. Blanca, the only *dama*, torn between her desire to be obedient to her father and her love for Juan, is spared further anguish when she beholds the perfidy of her lover. The ending also has a different twist: Not only does the chief *galán* not get his lady, but Tristán, his servant, marries Blanca's maid and Tristán remarks that this is the first *comedia* in which the servant marries and the master does not.

The play is classified as a *comedia* of magic, but it differs significantly from the others of this group. In *The Cave of Salamanca*, *The Stratagem at Melilla*, and *The Antichrist*, the effects and the illusion of the supernatural must be done through stage-craft, but in *The Test of Promises,* the action is similar to that of any *comedia de enredo* or intrigue. Only through the words of Don Illán toward the end of the play does the audience or reader realize that all that occurred was an illusion created by Don Illán:

> Then did you really think
> that you were marquis and president
> and favorite? All were
> fantastic illusions,
> which in the one hour of time
> that it took Pérez to prepare
> "Son of Fire"
> my science presented to you
> without [your] leaving this room.

> (*¿Luego tuvistes por cierto*
> *ser marqués y presidente*
> *y privado? Todas fueron*
> *fantásticas ilusiones,*
> *que en sola un hora de tiempo*
> *que tardó en adereçar*
> *Pérez el Hijo de Fuego,*
> *os respresentó mi ciencia*
> *sin salir deste aposento.*) (vv. 2684–92)

Perhaps mindful of the watchful eye of the Church, Alarcón takes pains to have Don Illán point out to Juan that the knowledge of black magic is permissible, but that teaching or practicing it is not.

The date of the play is given by Frank O. Reed,[46] Castro Leal (p. 140), and Bruerton as 1618, based on verses 2042–45 which describe a man who went to bed bald and next morning had a head covered with hair. The allusion is believed to be to Cristóbal Suárez de Figueroa, who is referred to as being bald and who had written in a work published the year before about a man who went to bed and woke up a *"don,"* a criticism of Alarcón's assuming this title. Alarcón may have had this in mind when he had Tristán assume the title of *"don,"* but the technical maturity of the comedy and the fact that it did not appear in the first volume suggest a date of composition somewhat later than 1618.

Fernández-Guerra (p. 263) thought the work the result of *oculto resentimiento* (hidden resentment) and indignation against powerful favorites and their worthless promises, but the tone of the work does not seem to support this. Alarcón takes some good-humored jabs at certain excesses, particularly in the scene of Act III in which Tristán, acting for Don Juan, is interviewing jobseekers. The protagonist, anything but admirable, bears his own name of Juan. To him also, he has Lucía falsely attribute certain defects (bad breath, etc.) of which he himself was accused, and he makes light of the criticism to which he was subjected when he added to his name the title "*don.*" Most critics give the play little notice. It deserves much better.

X   Los pechos privilegiados (Privileged Breasts)

For this play, which might also be entitled *The Ennobled Breasts,* Alarcón chose two insignificant incidents, unrelated except for their connection with Alfonso V, who ruled Asturias and León from 994 to 1027, and incorporated them in a work that developed two favorite themes of his, one the incorruptible and loyal vassal who suffers disgrace and misfortune through the scheming of one less scrupulous, and the other that of a ruler who seems to have had nothing else to occupy his mind and his time than to lust after the daughter, other relative, or bride-to-be, of a loyal subject. Alfonso's father died when his son was only five years of age and the boy was reared and prepared for the throne by the Count of Galicia, Melendo González, and his wife. They ruled in his stead wisely and faithfully and when Alfonso was of age to succeed to the throne, "in order that his tutors might have more authority, and in return for what they had done in his rearing and in the government," he married their daughter, Doña Elvira.[47]

A second incident is related by Fernández-Guerra (pp. 330–31) to the effect that among the counselors of the Indies was one Hernando de Villagómez from whom Alarcón one night heard the story that the wet nurses of his family were "privileged with a title of nobility," which must have been the result of "a very great deed." This extraordinary honor was said to have been granted by Alfonso V, and "even today [seventeenth century], the house of Villagómez has this privilege in its blason" (vv. 2839–41). Besides Alfonso, Doña Elvira, and her father, Melendo, the only other historical character is King Don Sancho of Navarra, who ascended the throne in the year 1000, ruled until 1035, "and was so outstanding in all manner of virtues" that he received the title of "The Great" (*el mayor*);[48] Alarcón depicts him as a man of honorable conduct, in contrast with Alfonso. Rodrigo de Villagómez, the protagonist, is a fictitious ancestor of the Villagómez family. Bermudo, the son of Melendo, may have been suggested by the fact that the son and heir of Alfonso and Elvira bore this name.

The play is one of the later ones of its author and its date of composition has been variously placed from 1619–1621? (by Castro Leal, p. 158) to 1620?–1625? (Bruerton). It was published in the eighteenth century with the title of *Nunca mucho costó poco* (*Much never Costs a Little*), and a play of this title, but completely different in content, was published as Lope's in the same spurious 22nd volume as the first edition of *The Truth Suspect*.[49]

The plot goes off in several directions. The main theme deals with Rodrigo de Villagómez, who is both a loyal favorite of his king and a man of integrity. He wishes in all ways to be obedient to his lord's command, but when he is asked to aid the king in his efforts to break down the resistance of Elvira for the sovereign's pleasure, he balks. Elvira loves the king, but her honor comes first and she refuses to submit to him. Not only is the king committed to marriage with a princess of Castile and his intentions toward Elivra, therefore, are not honorable, but Rodrigo is a good friend of Elvira's father and in love with his other daughter, Leonor, a combination of circumstances which creates a struggle between loyalty, friendship, virtue, and love. Angry at Rodrigo's prudishness, and thinking that he may himself be in love with Elvira, the king dismisses him and gets a favorite more amenable to his desires, one Ramiro, who is promised Leonor, Rodrigo's intended, as a reward. In order to escape the king's displeasure and retain his own self-respect, Rodrigo retires to his estate, Valmadrigal, to which Melendo and his family also repair so that Elvira may avoid the king's attentions. Alfonso follows, but the vigilance of Rodrigo and Melendo, the arrival of Sancho of Navarra, and the physical efforts of Jimena, the good-hearted but rough and powerful ("herculean," Fernández-Guerra calls her) former wet nurse of Rodrigo, frustrate the plans of Alfonso and his favorite, Ramiro. Eventually the jumbled pieces fall into place: Alfonso, basically a good fellow, marries Elvira, gives the Princess of Castile to Sancho, restores Rodrigo to favor, and permits him to marry Leonor. Finally, in order to justify the title, he grants the privilege of nobility to Jimena and her descendants because her breasts once nursed such a noble and valorous man as Rodrigo.

This play is one of the more popular of Alarcón. Perhaps it is because, as Castro Leal says (pp. 160–61), the first act is the best and the whole act is a "splendid beginning of one of those *comedias* which we have called heroic . . . ," or as Fernández-Guerra writes (p. 331), "in none of the Alarconian dramas is there a greater treasure of experience, more lofty thoughts, more profound statements, a more correct and elegant style, even if the plan and development of the story may be somewhat defective." The basic theme is, indeed, attractive and well developed: the triumph of good over evil, unswerving loyalty rewarded, and a king whose unscrupulousness is but a temporary lapse. But the inclusion of Jimena, likable as she is as a character, is unexpected, unnecessary, and not a little ridiculous. Her physical subjection of the king and later her defense of him are lacking in dignity, but in spite of her small and interruptive role, Jimena is probably the character who stands out in any reading of the play. She is the only example of the type in Alarcón, although the mannish woman is not unknown in the works of his contemporaries. She is presented as good, honest, tender in her affection for Rodrigo, fierce in her loyalty to her king, large, powerful, and of quaint and picturesque speech. Rodrigo is one of the most admirably upright characters that Alarcón has portrayed. Elvira is a vigorous, honorable lady, who, even though she loves the king, is unwilling to lose her self-respect. She leaves little for her sister, Leonor, to do, and the *dama* who is to be Rodrigo's wife is unfortunately a rather shadowy, docile figure. Melendo is presented as a man in great difficulty, mindful of his obligation to his lord and yet concerned about the honor of his family.

XI   La crueldad por el honor (Cruelty for the Sake of Honor)

In the year 1134, the King of Aragón, Don Alfonso I, disappeared in a battle against the Moors, and the fact that his body was never found gave rise to several rumors, among them one that, "tired of living, the battle having been lost," he went to Jerusalem. Having no children, Alfonso left his kingdoms to several military orders. This did not sit well either with the nobles of the realm or with his brother, Ramiro, who, in spite of having become a monk nearly forty years before, and of having been more recently elected Bishop of Roda and Barbastro, laid claim to the throne. He married, "whence resulted another marvel, to be for one person monk, priest, bishop, husband, and king," and a daughter, Petronila, was born of the union in 1135. Ramiro later contracted a marriage for her with Count Ramón Berenguer and retired once more to a monastery. Petronila had one son, who ascended the throne as Alfonso II in 1164, upon the abdication of his mother. Two years earlier, there had appeared an impostor who claimed that he was Alfonso I. He had, he said, spent much time in the Holy Land. His knowledge of the real Alfonso, the similarity of their features, the dissatisfaction of the nobles with a woman's rule (Ramón had just died), and the gullibility of the common herd, promised success, but he was exposed and executed later in the same year, "the reward for the scheme and the end of all this disagreeable tragedy." [50] Around this bit of history, Alarcón composed another play with the theme of a man who retires from his associates and disguises himself until the day when he can get revenge for an affront that has been done him, but whereas in *The Weaver of Segovia* Fernando Ramírez solves his problems satisfactorily, Aulaga of *Cruelty for the Sake of Honor* comes to a violent end.

The play was written in 1621 or 1622 according to Bruerton and possibly a year earlier according to Castro Leal (p. 170). Although Father Mariana does not name the imposter, Alarcón makes him a noble, Nuño Aulaga, who discovered that his wife, Teodora, had had relations with another man, Bermudo, prior to their marriage. Unwilling to publicize his shame, he is determined, as a man responsive to his *pundonor* (sense of honor), to cleanse this blemish on the family name. Queen Petronila, Prince Alfonso, and some of the lesser characters are either historical or have some historical basis.

In the play, Nuño, as a loyal vassal, had joined Alfonso I in his battle against the Moors and was with the king when he was killed. He buried him, retaining his ring and other indentifications, then, unable to face the shame that awaited him at home, he became a pilgrim, and now claims that he has come from the Holy Land and is on his way to Santiago de Compostela. He learns from Pedro Ruiz de Azagra that the kingdom of Aragón is

in turmoil. Queen Petronila wants to retire in favor of her young
son, but the nobles insist that she marry one of them and continue
to reign. Seeing his opportunity, Nuño declares that he is the long-
lost king, and produces identification. This, his intimate knowledge of Alfonso, and the fact that the twenty-eight years that have
elapsed have dulled the recollection of the real Alfonso's appearance, convince Pedro and he swears to follow him. In the palace
at Zaragoza, Petronila, like Penelope, is having difficulty fending
off the importunities of the several men who want her to marry
one of them or one of their sons. Among her subjects, only Sancho
Aulaga, son of the vanished Nuño, although the least in rank, is
her loyal supporter. Thus when the news of "Alfonso's" return arrives, the nobles, all except Sancho, angered at Petronila's stub-
bornness, desert her and swear allegiance to "Alfonso."

The imposter is at first successful even to the point of forcing
his son and Petronila to swear allegiance to him; Sancho, although
he is the only one aware of the true identity of the "king," does so
because the title of king is enough in itself to inspire obedience.
Inwardly, he is horrified and distressed that his father, whom he
should honor as parent and as king, is in fact a traitor. Through an
unexpected eavesdropping, the usurper is exposed and condemned to be hanged. Sancho visits him in prison and gives him a
dagger with which to kill himself. But suicide is a sin and to die
on the gallows, ignominious. Nuño orders Sancho to kill him and
Sancho, protesting, but obedient to his father's command and
mindful of the shame that his manner of death will bring to the
family, embraces his father and stabs him. Back at court it is
learned that Sancho is not the son of Nuño after all, but of Teodora
and Bermudo, who consents to marry her. Thus Sancho not only is
not guilty of patricide, but has also rid his country of a traitor and
remained loyal to his queen. During the play, Sancho has been
enamored of Teresa, but since she is the daughter of his real
father and a wife now dead, the marriage is impossible and she
is given to another suitor, Berenguel. With peace restored, the boy
Alfonso is proclaimed king and Petronila is permitted to abdicate.

Except for the introduction of the change in Sancho's paternity,
which seems unnecessarily contrived, *Cruelty for the Sake of
Honor* is an impressive play. Alarcón has expertly handled his historical source and adapted this insignificant twelfth-century episode to the requirements of a seventeenth-century *comedia* by

changing the chief motivation from a political one to one of honor, and the struggle between honor, loyalty, obedience, and love is skillfully done. Castro Leal (p. 171) and others have called it a *comedia heroica* (heroic *comedia*), but in general it has been ignored by critics. This may be because of the ending, which is both brutal and artificial. Castro Leal (pp. 173–74) criticizes the sudden invention of a different father for Sancho as superfluous and an error, so that "the thread of an eleventh-hour paternity only weakens the dramatic bond of the plot." He attributes this "invention" to a desire on Alarcón's part to explain that a man with the nobility and character of Sancho could not descend from a man like Nuño, but this does not seem to be so. Nuño, if misguided, is brave, a man of honor, and possessed of a certain dignity. Bermudo, the real father, does not impress with these qualities and his treatment of Sancho's mother, seducing her, then declining to marry her because of his concern with his position in court, and finally allowing her to languish in a convent during the twenty-odd years of Nuño's absence, do not describe a man who would father a person of Sancho's worth. It would seem, rather, that Alarcón, having settled the honor part of his plot, had second thoughts about portraying a son murdering his father, but in making the change, he blunted the impact of the title. That of a Dutch adaptation expresses the central theme a little more accurately: *The Punishment for Seeking a Crown.*[51]

The most interesting character, perhaps, is Nuño himself, a man whose sense of conjugal honor is so strong that he even stoops to become an imposter and to overthrow his lawful sovereign in an effort to achieve his revenge. For all the treachery of his intent, he remains a character of dignity and, even, sympathy. The most impressive character, however, is his "son," who is torn between several conflicting forces: love, honor, loyalty to his queen, and obedience to his "father." Alarcón vividly presents this conflict in a young man who, unlike many *galanes,* *has* to make a decision; the obstacles do not simply fall away as so often happens in the *comedia.* Unaware at the time that Nuño is not his father, he must nerve himself to slay him for the honor of his parent and his family name. He must also readjust his emotions and his thinking when he learns that the girl he loves is really his half-sister. Other *galanes* lose the girl they court through their own misbehavior, but the denial of Teresa to Sancho is beyond his control. The two

women, Teresa and Petronila, are admirable. In her intention of
disobeying her father and eloping with Sancho, not yet aware of
their relationship, Teresa, if unwise, at least shows initiative.

As in another play with political overtones, *The Master of the
Stars*, Alarcón introduces some ideas about laws. In Act III,
Zaratán, the *gracioso* and the first character to see Nuño Aulaga
upon his return, like Sancho Panza, wants a government and gives
Nuño, now Alfonso I, a list of some twelve laws that he would like
to see enacted. They are partly humorous and include such requirements that the lawyer of the loser pay all costs, thus inviting
fewer suits and more care on the lawyer's part; that the first pro-
duce should be cheaper and the later, when it is riper and better,
more expensive; that the sons of farmers and artisans be forbidden to study letters in view of the scarcity of these laborers; that
taxes should not be levied on the necessities of life, only on luxu-
ries ("those that are voluntary"); that men not have posts that
women can fill, for a man should be a soldier or farmer and "it is
not right that he sell silk or thread seated in a shop"; and others of
this nature, which in spite of the humor, contain a germ of truth
and perhaps even a touch of bitterness, such as that His Majesty
should sell positions and offices, "since there will be a thousand to
buy them" (Alarcón had not yet received the position to which he
felt he was entitled and which he had been seeking for at least
eight years). He also suggests, since there was much complaint in
Alarcón's day about women who went about veiled, that only
prostitutes be permitted to go about the streets *tapadas* (veiled);
the pure and chaste would then be eager to go about undisguised.
This moment for the *gracioso*, although only tenuously relevant to
the plot, is the one digression of any consequence in the work.[52]

XII   Examen de maridos (Examination of Husbands)

The last of the plays that Alarcón published and possibly the
last that he wrote deals with the means adopted by a lady for
choosing the best man for a husband from among her several suitors. Her decision to conduct an examination or evaluation of those
who would marry her is made because of an admonition of her
recently-deceased father: *Antes que te cases, mira lo que haces*
("before you marry, watch what you are doing"), a *refrán* or
proverb, which has served as an alternate title to the work.

The plot itself seems to be Alarcón's own, although Castro Leal

(p. 181) suggests that the idea of reviewing a list of possible candidates may have been suggested by a play attributed to Tirso de Molina, and there also comes to mind the "casket scene" of *The Merchant of Venice* in which the future husband will be he who chooses the correct casket. Carl D. Anderson discusses a number of works with elements similar to *Examen de maridos* (*Examination of Husbands*), but they are, he points out, elements which were common to literature of that period and earlier: "It may be stated that Alarcón does not owe much to any of the works, . . . nor does it seem that subsequent writers adopted from him much more than the general theme . . ." [53] *Examination of Husbands* has been dated 1622–1623? by Castro Leal (p. 181). Fernández-Guerra (p. 417) chose 1625, Bruerton 1623?–1625. Hartzenbusch (p. xi) says only that it is before 1631. All, then, agree that it is a late play. It is one of his plays mentioned by Alarcón that became part of the plumage of other "crows," since it was first published as a work of Lope de Vega in the spurious 24th part of his *comedias* (Zaragoza, 1633). [54] The version that Alarcón published differs from it somewhat, particularly in some corrections and in the suppression of verses. These changes are generally attributed to Alarcón's effort to polish the play before publication. [55] The setting is the Madrid of Alarcón's time.

The story is a simple one. Having been convinced that she must choose a husband, but mindful of her father's advice, Doña Inés decides to note and examine the claims and qualifications of a large number of *galanes*. For some time she has been courted by Don Carlos, but she does not like him; she is, however, attracted to the Marquis Fadrique. In the course of the play the competition is narrowed to these two and it is to be decided by a debate, the winner to have the hand of Inés. An earlier love of Fadrique, in jealousy, spreads a false rumor about various physical defects that Fadrique has as well as one that she has been in love with Carlos for a long time. The subject of the debate is whether a lady should marry the man she loves with all his faults or marry a more perfect specimen, whom she does not love. Carlos argues the former and is declared winner, but since it is his argument that won, he yields to Fadrique and takes for himself the unknown (to him) lady who has said that she was in love with him.

The play remains among Alarcón's most popular and best-known productions. Millares Carlo [56] writes that "when one speaks

of the *comedia* of character of the Mexican dramatist, there come
to mind and to the points of the pen his two masterworks: *The
Walls Have Ears* and *The Truth Suspect*. But read *Examination
of Husbands* and it will be seen—we believe—that it does not
yield in perfection, beauty, and ability of construction to the
works which are considered the best and most famous of our author." There are some exceptions, but the majority of critics have
praised the work very highly and it is one of the most frequently
printed of his *comedias*.[57]

It is well constructed, and Alarcón maintains to the very end
the suspense as to whom Inés will finally wed. The characters are
among the better drawn of Alarcón. Doña Inés is of the type of
Doña Ana de Contreras of *The Walls Have Ears*, capable, considerate, and practical, except in matters of love, when emotion takes
hold. Blanca is cast in the mold of certain *damas* of Alarcón's
earlier plays. Like Julia of *The Resembler of Himself*, she is unin-
terested in her suitor until he wants to leave her, and then she seeks
revenge in a rather vile way. The peculiar, almost mechanical, attitude toward love, marriage, and friendship is well demonstrated in
this *comedia*. Blanca dislikes the marquis because of his poverty,
likes him when he becomes rich and seeks another, pretends to like
a man (Carlos) whom she has not met, and then accepts him when
he offers his hand. Fadrique abandons Blanca and is willing even
to give up Inés when he finds that his interest in these women
conflicts with his friendship for Carlos. Carlos, in spite of his persistent wooing of Inés suddenly gives up and begins courting
Blanca, because his chivalrous nature feels sorry for a lady who,
he thinks, has secretly been pining for him for several years. Inés
is the most consistent; she has never loved Carlos and she does
love Fadrique for all his "defects," but having committed herself
to accepting the results of the debate, she is willing to marry Carlos even though she does not love him. In a sense the title is misleading. Although the play promises a practical and reasoned approach to marriage, it ends similarly to many another *comedia,*
with Alarcón's frequent introduction of a surprise element, here
the sacrifice of Carlos.

CHAPTER 4

The Attributed Plays and Minor Works

I Plays in Collaboration

BESIDES those plays that Alarcón himself published in 1628 and 1634, and which he claimed were all his, several other *comedias* have been attributed to him with various degrees of probability, and in a number of others he is said to have collaborated. The only example of certain collaboration is *Algunas hazañas de las muchas de don García Hurtado de Mendoza, marqués de Cañete,* (*supra* p. 28). As a dramatic work it is worth little, and Alarcón's contribution, the first scene of Act II, is no better and no worse than the remainder. Besides this and the notorious *Descriptive Panegyric,* there is no definite evidence that he joined forces with any of his contemporaries in any other work. He is said to have produced parts of such plays as *Cautela contra cautela* (*Cunning for Cunning*), of unknown authorship although included in the *Segunda parte* (*Second Volume*) of the *comedias* of Tirso de Molina; *La villana de Vallecas* (*The Village Girl of Vallecas*), definitely a work by Tirso, and *Próspera fortuna de don Álvaro de Luna* (*Prosperous Fortune of Don Alvaro de Luna*). Of the first, Hartzenbusch (p. vii) wrote that "it has several scenes which seem to be Tirso's and others, which, for me, were undoubtedly written by Alarcón." Fernández-Guerra (p. 299) also thought it a collaboration of Tirso and Alarcón, but as Professor Morley showed (p. 147) years ago, the association rests entirely on style and there is nothing in the versification to support or deny the claims for Alarcón's contribution. Millares Carlo (III, xv) rejects it. Alarcón's association with the second and the third is even more tenuous. The burden of proof lies on those who make the claim and unless this proof is forthcoming, and it has not been until now, they cannot be considered a product of Alarcón's pen.

Siempre ayuda la verdad (*The Truth Always Helps*) is also one of the plays of Tirso's *Segunda parte,* which appeared in 1635, one

91

year after the publication of Alarcón's own *Segunda parte*. Fernández-Guerra gives a fanciful account of its origin as a work begun by Alarcón, completed by Luis Belmonte Bermúdez (who had collaborated in *Algunas hazañas*), polished by the two, and done at the request of the Marquis of Cañete for presentation at the palace in 1623.[1] Castro Leal (p. 177), although admitting the possibility of a different collaborator, including Tirso, believes that Alarcón wrote part of it: "There are scenes so fitting the Alarconian style that it is difficult to believe that he did not write them." Francisco Medel del Castillo, in his catalogue of titles of *comedias*, published in 1735, lists a play with this title by Alarcón, but this title could apply equally well to *The Truth Suspect*.[2] Although Hamilton (p. 129) finds nothing against Alarcón's authorship in the epistolary portion, Morley (p. 147) believes that it is unlikely that Alarcón wrote the entire play in view of the small percentage of his favorite meter, the *redondilla*. It is extremely doubtful that Alarcón had any hand in its composition.

II   *Plays of Doubtful Attribution*

Of plays that have been attributed entirely to Alarcón, we have already rejected two as not by him: *The Weaver of Segovia*, Part One (*supra*, p. 78), and *Who Deceives Whom Most* (*supra*, p. 58, n. 26). Another attributed to him, this time by Fernández-Guerra (p. 415), because of what he believes to be similarities between it and *The Antichrist*, is *El condenado por desconfiado* (*The Man Damned for Distrusting*), which also appeared in Tirso's second volume. Professor Morley (p. 149) does not believe that Tirso wrote the play as it stands and is certain that Alarcón did not in view of the low percentage of *redondillas*, a verse form of which Alarcón was inordinately fond.

Although the remaining three plays have been attributed to Alarcón since their earliest extant printing, the first known edition of each is dated after his death. The first is *La culpa busca la pena y el agravio la venganza* (*Guilt Seeks Punishment and Insult, Vengeance*), the earliest known text of which is dated 1646.[3] Fernández-Guerra, calling it "more disorganized and less well written" than his other plays, thought it either an early effort (about 1611) or the result of still another collaboration, for either of which reasons Alarcón could have decided not to include it in the first volume of his plays. Castro Leal (pp. 77–78) states that it "evidently is one of his first dramatic efforts," written perhaps in Mexico and "touched up" before its performance in Madrid. He blames the vitiated state of the text on the possibility that it was carried around in the trunk of some impresario. It is understandable that the play would suffer if indeed it was carried about from around 1599 (the date Hartzenbusch assigns to it), or even 1611, to 1646, either in Alarcón's luggage or in that of an "impresario." It is surprising that it survived at all.

The plot concerns a young man, Rodrigo, whose life has been saved by a certain Don Fernando, with whose sister he falls in love. But it turns out that Fernando had once insulted the father of Rodrigo and the family honor requires that vengeance be taken. This conflict between love, honor, and oblgation (or gratitude or friendship) is complicated by subelements, but is finally resolved when Rodrigo challenges and kills Fernando, thus eliminating the odd man, permitting two couples to marry, and satisfying the honor of Don Antonio.

Professor Morley, in his tabulation of the strophic practice of Alarcón (pp. 134, 140) includes *Guilt Seeks Punishment* among the authentic plays and gives forty-five percent and forty-five and one-half percent, respectively, for *redondillas* and *romance*. In the authentic plays, the percentage of *redondilla* ranges from forty to eighty-two, but the highest for *romance* is only forty-one. Castro Leal writes of the play (p. 78):

It preserves, in spite of the retouching, the most characteristic defects of a dramatic apprentice: the excessively long speeches and the abundance of unnecessary asides. The style is diffuse; the characters do not succeed in finding, after delayed intent, the expressions suitable for refining their situation or their feelings. The action, as with every beginner, is overloaded with incidents. Neither in the motives which inspire its plot, nor in its conception and construction, nor even in its style is there a single indication that might reveal the distinctive qualities of Alarcón.

And this from a scholar who accepts the play as his. In *The Resembler of Himself* (vv. 2158–60) is the adage, *el que la culpa comete,/la pena quiere llevar* ("he who commits a wrong, will bear the punishment"). Perhaps the "moral" tone of the title and the similarity of these verses to it may account for assigning the work to Alarcón.

III   Quien mal anda en mal acaba (He Who Follows
an Evil Way, Ends in an Evil Way)

Quien mal anda en mal acaba is a more interesting work. The earliest known edition is a seventeenth-century *suelta*, printed in Sevilla by Francisco de Leefdael. Castro Leal (p. 80) believes that the play was written very early, (1601–1603?) while the news of the trial on which it is based was still fresh. Fernández-Guerra (pp. 119–20) believes that Alarcón was reminded of the incident and inspired to write the play because of a "famous" *auto de fe* (burning of heretics at the stake) which occurred in 1616, and places the date at 1617.[4]

In 1599, there was held, in Cuenca, a trial by the Inquisition of one Román Ramírez, who was of Moorish descent and at the time sixty years old. He cultivated the fields of the Duke of Medinaceli, who because of suits he brought against his neighbors, antagonized them against himself and Román. The Moor also practiced medicine, but only when asked to. He was said to have made a pact with the devil and then bewitched a woman of Soria, later "curing" her. His own defense was that he treated her with herbs, an art that he had learned from his mother. He admitted that his grandfather had spoken with the devil and that he also could do so after his grandfather's death. The trial began in 1599, and although Román took ill and died in December of that year, it was continued until he was condemned, his bones exhumed and burned, and his property confiscated.[5]

The plot follows the known facts of Román Ramírez to some extent. It takes place in Deza, the home of Román, and tells of his love for Doña Aldonza, who, however, abhors him. When he expresses a desire for her, the devil appears, ready to help him, and in the resulting pact, he becomes a doctor, with the devil as his assistant. He first causes Doña Aldonza to find her suitor, Don Juan, a repulsive person (according to the trial records, the lady Román treated rejected her husband). Juan calls upon Román to treat her for a mysterious illness, and Aldonza begins to take a liking to her doctor. Román is eager to possess Aldonza, but his devil advises patience and has Román appear as Don Diego de Guzmán. She falls in love with Diego, and their marriage is arranged, but as it is about to take place, two representatives of the

Inquisition appear and arrest "Don Diego" as a heretic and wizard. Explanations are made and Aldonza returns to Don Juan.

Castro Leal (p. 82) states that it is the first dramatic treatment of the idea of a pact with a devil in Spain, but this is true only if we assume a composition before 1612, for in this year there appeared *El esclavo del demonio* (*The Slave of the Devil*), a more famous play on the theme, by Antonio Mira de Amescua. However, the idea had already occurred in Spanish literature in such works as Juan Manuel's 45th *ejemplo,* in which a man makes a pact with the devil in order to recover the wealth that he had lost. He is able to steal with impunity, but loses his life in the end. The same theme appears in Gonzalo de Berceo's 25th *milagro,* or miracle, of the Virgin.

Professor Morley (pp. 138–40) includes the play among the authentic ones of Alarcón and does not question its authenticity, but he does note the low percentage of *romance,* six percent; the lowest in an authentic play is fourteen percent. Hamilton (p. 132) concludes from his study of Alarcón's use of letters that the play, "differing from Alarcón's usages only with its broken *redondillas,* probably is his work." There are Alarconian elements in the *comedia:* the high percentage of *redondilla,* the little variation in strophes (only four), the interest in magic, the use of a historical episode around which to weave a *comedia,* and the introduction of an episode used twice elsewhere, that of describing someone's violent death only to have the "dead" man show up. Alarcón may have written this play. It would be nice to know for certain, and why it was not included among those published by him.

IV No hay mal que por bien no venga (It's an Ill Wind that Blows No Good)

This *comedia,* more literally translated *There Is No Evil that May Not Come for Good,* also appeared after the death of Alarcón, in the *Laurel de comedias. Qvarta parte de diferentes avtores* (*Laurel of comedias. Fourth Volume of Different Authors*), published in Madrid in 1653. It has always been attributed to Alarcón without question, included among his best productions, and is, indeed, a splendid work, but it presents a puzzle as to when it was written and why it was not included among the twenty that he published, to many of which it is greatly superior.

Like other plays of the Mexican, it is based on a historical episode, in addition to which a title has been chosen from the *refranero* or collection of proverbs. The source again is Padre Mariana
(p. 217):

For such great and so many works [construction and reconstruction as
the country was recovering from the Moors] the royal treasury or
estates were not sufficient; [the King, Alfonso III] imposed new taxes,
something that should always be avoided, unless it is when the republic
is in such straits, for all understand that it is necessary to subject themselves to need if they wish to be saved. This truth is better understood
because of what resulted. The vassals were, for this reason, unhappy;
the Queen Doña Jimena [of Aragón, whom Alfonso had married in
877], who was also displeased with her husband, persuaded Don
García, her son, to take advantage of that occasion and take up arms
against his father. The King was not taken unawares; although old and
weak, he hastened to Zamora, seized his son and ordered him guarded
in the castle of Gauzón. The bitterness and evils did not cease at this.
The father-in-law of Don García was Nuño Hernández, Count of
Castile, a powerful prince in wealth and in vassals. He, with the help
of the Queen and of the [two] brothers of the prisoner, made fierce
war against the King, which lasted two years. At the end of them the
conspirators succeeded in their intent and the poor King, tired of the
task or desirous of a calmer life, renounced his kingdom and gave it to
his son García.

This occurred in 910 and Alfonso died in Zamora the following
year. It is satisfying to record that García enjoyed his ill-gotten
kingdom only three years, dying in 914.

With this as the point of departure, the author has constructed
a play with one of the most unusual characters in the *comedia,*
Don Domingo de Don Blas. Don Juan Bermúdez, of noble blood
but twisted ethics, has spent all of his estate in wooing Leonor.
She loves him in spite of his unsavory reputation, but her father
Ramiro cannot stand him. Ramiro, who might well be modeled
after Nuño Hernández (a servant bears the name Nuño in the
play), is important, rich, and miserly. Don Juan rents a house
(which he does not own) to Don Domingo de Don Blas, a truly
eccentric *galán,* which is next door to that of Ramiro. When Don
Domingo discovers that Juan does not own the house and he has
to pay his rent again to the real owner, he calls Juan a "thief, a
trickster, a subtle Cacus" in the presence of Leonor. The *dama's*

affection for Juan evaporates and Juan, himself, however much a scoundrel he may be, does not like this insult to his "honor," and challenges Don Domingo to a duel. These scenes and the idiosyncrasies of Don Domingo as to dress, food, and shelter, make for a hilarious beginning, but in Act II the work takes a serious turn.

Prince García is preparing the revolt against his father and is lining up the most influential citizens of Zamora on his behalf. The greedy Ramiro joins readily, but complications arise when Don Domingo refuses to aid García. Lest he reveal the plot, Domingo is imprisoned in Ramiro's house. Meanwhile, Juan is pursuing his larcenous way and plans to enter the house of Ramiro secretly and steal his hoarded treasure. Instead of treasure, he comes upon Domingo, who tells the whole story and asks Juan to alert the king, who arrives in time to arrest his son, and imprison him. Domingo is freed and marries the cousin of Leonor. The king ignores Ramiro's part in the conspiracy so that the shame of treason will not fall upon Leonor, and she is thus able to marry Juan who has redeemed himself through his efforts to aid his sovereign.

The play has many Alarconian features. There are the typical complaints of *pobreza* (poverty), the stress on the loyalty owing to one's monarch, the triumph of good over evil, and the introduction of a *cuento* (or story) by the *gracioso* to illustrate a point.[6] Another incident is reminiscent of *The Truth Suspect:* the explanation of Don Domingo's curious *apellido* (family name) of Don Blas, taken to please a childless uncle who had left him his estate. In *The Truth Suspect*, García forgets the name of his supposed father-in-law and when caught giving him two, explains that he is known by both, one before he received an inheritance and the other after; "this situation is not novel in many houses of Spain" (*no es nueva esa condición/en muchas casas de España*), replies Beltrán (vv. 2272–73). Ramiro's dislike of Juan's *degeneración de su nobleza* (deterioration of his nobility) expressed to the prince is similar to Beltrán's words of reproof to his son García in *The Truth Suspect* and those of the marquis to his son, Juan, in *The Weaver of Segovia.*

Hamilton (p. 126) found that the epistolary practice of the play corresponded "to Alarcón's known customs in all respects except for the broken stanza in the letter which is read aloud," and Professor Morley's study of his versification (p. 136) shows no significant deviation from Alarcón's habits, even though no authentic play by him contains such a high proportion of *silvas* (36 verses). Act II is written entirely in *redondillas,* as are Act I of *The Entanglement of a Deception* and, except for eighteen verses of a *balada* or song, all of Act III of *The Antichrist.*

The late professor Mabel M. Harlan, in her edition, suggests the dates 1631 or 1632 as "a likely date of composition, . . . which was perhaps its author's 'swan song' for the stage" and Adolfo Bonilla y San Martín, who also edited the work, says only "after the beginnings of 1623," the year in which the *golilla,* mentioned in Act I, was first worn.[7] This was a collar of such proportions and construction that to put it on was "like putting one's head in a stock, a torture inexcusable in Spain." [8] In the play reference is also made to a jackdaw who dressed himself in the feathers of other birds, a reminder of Alarcón's complaint that his plays had been the plumage of other crows.[9] Alarcón made a similar remark in the preface to the edition of 1634 and referred specifically to two plays which had appeared in 1630 and 1632 or 1633, respectively. Thus, the play may have been written subsequent to 1632 or 1633, too late for inclusion in the second volume.

The play begins as a real comedy: The unscrupulousness of Juan, the eccentricity of Domingo, and the amusing reactions of the *damas.* The women are typically Alarconian in their lack of distinction, but the men are all well drawn. Don Domingo is an *acomodado,* whose sole concern in the beginning is his convenience. He wants comfortable clothes, regardless of style, wishes to eat when he is hungry, not when it is customary to do so, desires a house that is neither damp nor noisy. When he is invited to attend a *fiesta,* he wants to observe, not to be required to join in the bullfight,[10] and when he is ready to settle down, he wants his lady to marry right away so that he won't have the trouble of courting or the danger of catching cold while serenading. Yet all of this disappears when duty to country calls. Juan's, too, is a splendid sketch of a person whom poverty has made impervious to decency to such an extent that his future father-in-law, Ramiro, admittedly prejudiced, says that the only thing that he has not done is murder, and implies that he would do that if he thought he could conceal it. Interesting too, and very Alarconian, are the two servants, Nuño and Mauricio, of Don Domingo, whose concern for their master is more than the usual relationship between master and servant. It is Nuño's worry about Domingo's disappearance that eventually takes him to the prince himself for aid and justice against Juan, whom he suspects of having done away with his master.

V *Minor Works*

Besides his dramatic works, the only surviving pieces from Alarcón's pen are some occasional verses, which are only that— occasional, and mere versifying.[11] The earliest extant are those that he wrote for the Fiesta of San Juan de Alfarache (*supra*, pp. 19–20) and consist of one *redondilla* and four *décimas*, addressed to a lady whose hands perspired a great deal. Five years later, in 1611, the doctor Gutierre Marqués de Careaga published his book *Desengaño de la fortuna* (*Disillusionment of Fortune*), "very profitable and necessary for all manner of people and states," but with an *aprobación* (approval) as early as 1608 and a *dedicatoria* of Salamanca, May 15, 1607.[12] Alarcón's contribution, a *décima*, must have been composed prior to his departure for Mexico, since he was already there by the time the book appeared, a fact that suggests that his talents as a poet were being exercised and revealed as early as his student days. Besides praising Marqués de Careaga for having shown that letters have greater luck than arms, it is a play on the word *pluma* ("feather" and "pen"). Fernández-Guerra (p. 158) is not wrong in saying that "it does not add any worth or value to [Alarcón's] literary reputation."

In 1617, he contributed some laudatory verse, this time two *redondillas*, to a novel, *Los más fieles amantes* (*The Most Faithful Lovers*), *Leucipe y Clitifonte*, a Greek tale by Achilles Tatius, *traducida, censurada, y en parte compuesta* ("translated, censored, and in part composed") by Diego de Agreda y Vargas. The book is dedicated to Don Juan de Luna y Mendoza, Marqués de Montesclaros (at one time Viceroy of Mexico and, later, Peru), and other contributors include Doña Clara de Bobadilla y Alarcón and Doña Beatriz de Zúñiga y Alarcón, all members of the Alarcón and Mendoza families of which Alarcón himself was so proud and whose names he so often used for the characters of his plays. This verse is interesting also in that it is the first time that we have Alarcón signing himself with his full name and title, "el licenciado don Juan Ruiz de Alarcón y Mendoza."[13] The *redondillas* note

that the author has both "given life" to the original author and
deprived him of honor, since the new work is superior to the original.

The following year, there appeared two *quintillas*, in praise of
another new work, the *Proverbios morales y consejos cristianos
muy provechosos para concierto y espejo de la vida, adornado de
lugares y textos de las divinas y humanas letras, y enigmas filosó-
ficos naturales y morales, con sus comentos* (*Moral Proverbs and
Christian Advice, Very Profitable for the Harmony and Mirror of
Life, Embellished with Citations and Texts and Natural and
Moral Philosophical Enigmas, with Their Commentary*), a work
which is reflected in his play, *The Master of the Stars*, and which
appeared in Madrid in 1618. The author was at the time physician
to the Crown Prince, the future Felipe IV, and Alarcón praises the
manner in which he has prepared this "prescription" for his suffering (*doliente*) country, coating the advice with sweetness.

Still more dedicatory verse, two *redondillas*, were produced for
the publication of the second part of the *Poema trágico del español Gerardo y el desengaño del amor lascivo* (*Tragic Poem of the
Spaniard Gerardo and the Disillusionment of Lascivious Love*)
by Gonzalo de Céspedes y Meneses (1621 in Madrid, 1625 in Lis-
bon). In them Alarcón implies that Céspedes has pictured the
tragic end of love's passion so vividly that it appears to be a tragedy of love itself. They are, as Jiménez Rueda (p. 248) says, *bien
pobres* ("quite poor"). In the same year, upon the death on the
scaffold of the notorious Rodrigo Calderón, Alarcón composed an
epitaph in the form of a sonnet, which is "cold, faint, and obscure"
(Fernández-Guerra, p. 349). Also in the year 1621, he wrote two
sonnets in indignation at the destruction by Calvinists, in Prete of
the Lower Palatinate, of a figure of Christ Crucified, which the
Catholics were later able to restore. In the first he compares
the Calvinists with the infidels of Palestine and is consoled by the
knowledge that the Catholics have returned Christ to His cross,
the symbol of His triumph as well as the scene of His suffering.
The second laments the impiety of the destruction, since the
figure represents on earth the Divine Being, and praises the restoration of the figure. They contain the most intense religious feeling to be found anywhere in his works.

On the 21st of August, 1622, the Count of Villamediana was
assassinated in the Calle Mayor. He was notorious and hated for

his barbed satire, and his death elicited a number of uncomplimentary verses. The one from Alarcón is a *décima* quite in contrast with the philosophy of *The Walls Have Ears,* not to speak ill
of anyone: "Here lies a slanderer who spoke ill even of himself";
he died showing "how an evil deed succeeded in ending his
slander." Another *décima* was contributed to a collection of
twelve amorous short stories (*Novelas amorosas*) printed in Madrid in 1624 by an Italian, José Camerino. In this effort he praises
the *novelas* as giving "new thirst to desire" and states that his own
muse of Castilian poetry would be fortunate if she could equal the
prose of the Tuscan. It is a nicely turned bit of laudation.

On October 13, 1631, there was held a great celebration in the
palace gardens in honor of the two-year-old Crown Prince, Baltasar Carlos. It took the form of animal fights with a lion, tiger, bull,
camel, bear, horse, and others. The only survivor of this warped
idea of entertainment was the bull, which, as a reward for its
bravery and prowess, was given the questionable privilege of
being shot to death by the King himself, because "since he entered
the amphitheater to die, to pardon its life would be a punishment,
leaving it at the risk of losing it in some plebeian bullring or at
base hands." Alarcón contributed one sonnet to commemorate the
event and the seventh line of another written in collaboration
with "eight or nine" other wits.[14]

If Alarcón gave up the writing of plays after his assumption of
the post of *relator interino,* he continued to write verse when the
occasion beckoned. On December 16, 1631, the volcano Vesuvius
erupted and the event brought from Felipe IV a request to José
de Quiñones that he write about the event. Quiñones asked
twenty-three poets to embellish his work, which was published
the following year, 1632, in Madrid. Among them was Alarcón,
who contributed a sonnet, which refers to the volcano as the "unlucky son of the red planet" (that is Vulcan, son of Jupiter), and
warns that if this threat of heavenly ire is so disastrous, mortals
should look to themselves for when the final cataclysm occurs.
The subject may have appealed to Alarcón, for in some of his
plays he makes comparisons with volcanos, and there is a fine description of the similarity of the eruption of a volcano and the rise
of righteous indignation in the breast of Don Domingo in *It Is an
Ill Wind that Blows No Good* (whose conjectured date of composition is about the same time), when he learns of the plan to be-

tray the king. Fernández-Guerra (p. 449) considers this sonnet the last composition from Alarcón's pen and it may well be. In 1635, however, there appeared *Historia ejemplar de las dos constantes mugeres españolas* (*Exemplary History of the Two Constant Spanish Women*), a novel by Luis Pacheco de Narváez, a famous swordsman who was a fencing teacher of Felipe IV. The earliest *aprobación* (approval) however, is 1630, so that Alarcón had probably written by then the two *décimas* which he contributed to the *fajo* (bundle) of verses that prefaced it. The first comments on Pacheco's dexterity in fencing and his "constancy" in writing. The second remarks that although it is difficult to find even *one* firm (constant?) woman, Pacheco has created two.[15]

CHAPTER 5

The Man and His Work

THE preceding pages have touched on Alarcón's dramatic art, his use of sources, development of plot, and characterization. Here an attempt will be made to summarize the man in his art in a more general way.

I *Versification*

Alarcón was an unimaginative versifier. Although he uses almost all of the various strophes to be found in the *comedia* in general, many are used sparingly and most (over ninety percent) of the nearly fifty-eight thousand lines of verse of his authentic plays are octosyllabic, and of these, nearly sixty-five percent are in *redondillas*.[1] No act is without them and one play has one composed entirely in this meter. The preponderance of the *redondilla* is one of the most distinguishing features of his work. The octosyllable, the *redondilla* in particular, lends itself to rapid movement, sparkling conversation, and pithy statement, all characteristics of Alarcón's plays. It is perhaps not without significance that his most famous work, *The Truth Suspect*, has only seventy-three nonoctosyllabic verses, the smallest number in any authentic play.

In the use of strophes of Italian origin, with their hendecasyllabic (and occasionally heptasyllabic) lines, he was less adept and apparently found them less attractive for either his ability or his purpose. He uses the sonnet only nine times, twice in two plays and not at all in most of them. They are not very inspired, and in *The Walls Have Ears* he appears to be mocking the form, since he has Beltrán, the *gracioso*, add another tercet to the sonnet just recited by his master. Lamenting his lack of success with Doña Ana, Don Juan ends his sonnet:

> Sad, where it is necessary not to hope,
> where despairing is victory,
> where winning gives strength to the enemy.

> (*¡Triste, donde es el no esperar forzoso,*
> *donde el desesperar es la vitoria,*
> *donde el vencer da fuerza al enemigo!*) (vv. 328–30)

To this Beltrán replies:

> Sad, where it is necessary to go with you,
> where to find something to eat is victory,
> where eating supper is ever a memory.

> (*¡Triste, donde es forzoso andar contigo*
> *donde hallar que comer es gran vitoria,*
> *donde el cenar es siempre de memoria!*) (vv. 331–33)

In *The Test of Promises,* the sonnet, which is often in other playwrights a soliloquy by a distressed lover in a serious moment, is used for a conversation between two servants, although it is on the subject of love (vv. 1831–58).

More frequent for lyrical outbursts is the *lira,* which Alarcón uses in eight different plays, once in each, and in passages ranging from six to 120 lines. They are usually composed in a rather gongoristic manner, as befits their lyric purpose, to express love or indignation: Don Mendo addressing Doña Ana in *The Walls Have Ears,* Diana reproaching the king for his unchivalrous behavior in *Friendship Punished,* or Doña Ana seeking justice of Pedro the Cruel in *How to Win Friends.* In *The Antichrist,* Alarcón introduces but one strophe within a passage of *redondillas,* in which each of four people speaks twice, an incredible mangling of this attractive verse form.

Although Alarcón's metrics offer no great variety, and his verses are more correct than inspired, with few bursts of lyricism,[2] he was a competent poet and the results are not hackneyed. He is economical and careful, both in form and in vocabulary, and errors in construction, syntactical or metrical, are few.[3]

II   *Alarcón, The Careful Craftsman*

The care with which Alarcón prepared his compositions has frequently been stated, perhaps overstated. It has been written that he "wrote little, but carefully, polishing and improving without letup," that he is "almost the only dramatist of his time who seems to have ripened his compositions and polished them with care," that he "wrote little, put polished much," and that "the plays of his maturity, . . . show evidence of the greatest care in composition, and of conscientious and painstaking correction, even in small details, until he arrived at the adequate expression of precise thought." [4] Some of these opinions are based on the belief that the differences between the pirated editions of his plays and those authorized later by Alarcón himself reflect his efforts to polish his work, but in view of the abandon with which plays were plagiarized and pirated, the earlier variants may not be Alarcón's at all. Nevertheless, his work represents a finished product both in concept and in execution. Where the plot is a simple one, with but one *dama* and two *galanes* (*The Test of Promises*), there is no difficulty and the play moves with precision and directness, but even where the play is complicated by two plots, such as in *The Resembler of Himself*, and the affairs of one pair of lovers are distinct from those of the other, the primary and secondary intrigues come together and separate when appropriate, and are so skillfully interwoven that one does not obstruct the other. Even in such plays as *The Stratagem at Melilla* or *The Cave of Salamanca*, in which the simple plot risks becoming lost in the many extraneous elements introduced, Alarcón does not lose his grasp of plot or digressions.

His concern for detail is apparent in his efforts to justify or explain plausibly what is obviously an unlikely occurrence. An excellent example is the detail with which Don Juan of *The Resembler of Himself* explains how he intends to prepare for and carry out his plan. Similarly, there are scenes in which a character, in the presence of the audience, arrives at a point of view or explains a decision as a result of deliberation and deduction: Don Juan's explanation (in *Intrigue and Luck*) to Arnesto why he should not fear him as a rival and Fadrique's reasoning (in *Changing for the Better*) regarding the pleasures of courting a lady.

The playwright's correctness in versification, structure, and argument did not extend to other details. Anachronisms abound in his work as they do in that of all of his contemporaries; they were little bothered about historical and geographical exactness or local color, so that Alarcón has Calvin mentioned in the eleventh century and the capture of Granada in the fourteenth; localities of Madrid become part of "a city of Bohemia," and seventeenth-century ideas of honor are expressed in ancient Greece. He was also indifferent to the repetition of scenes, ideas, and even verses. He himself condemns a lack of variety in the *comedia*, "for it is bad for a poet not to vary, since the value lies in not repeating" (*que a un poeta le está mal/no variar, que el caudal/se muestra en no repetir*) (*The Walls Have Ears*, vv. 1191–93). There is similarity in development such as having one *dama* try to upset the marriage plans of another or having a member of a royal family pursue a *dama* solely for carnal purposes. There are similar scenes such as those in which a servant fails in his errand because he falls asleep after drinking or in which there is an attempt at forcible possession. Concepts are repeated such as "an angel in comprehension" (*The Walls Have Ears*, vv. 1468–71, and *Changing for the Better*, vv. 1688–89).[5] His annoyance at not getting the post he desired is reflected in two plays (*The Entanglements of a Deception* and *Friendship Punished*) in which not only the idea, but the words are identical. A character wishes for another a life that will be

> Longer than a tired minister's
> whom an unfortunate man
> expects to succeed.

> (*Más que un ministro cansado,*
> *de quien tiene un desdichado*
> *la futura sucesión*) (vv. 2119–21; 2208–10)

Such repetition does not mar the plays in any way and, indeed, the scenes, ideas, and expressions are quite apropos and effective when and where they are used, but the practice renders inaccurate the opinion of Hartzenbusch, repeated since then, of "his continual care for avoiding repetition." [6]

III *Alarcón as a* culteranista

One of the literary phenomena of the period in which Alarcón wrote was *culteranismo* (cultism or euphuism), found in other literatures as well as in that of Spain. Alarcón was essentially not a *culteranista*, and an extended discussion of this development is not appropriate here, but in brief, it was an artificial and affected, but inventive and colorful manner of writing. At first clever, and even beneficial to Spanish literary development, the movement eventually overreached itself and degenerated into the absurd and tasteless. Not all poets fell victim to the craze and some took occasion to make fun of it. Alarcón has been classified as an anticultist and, in fact, one would not expect from his practical and somewhat unimaginative mind what would be required for its practice. It may be remembered that he was unable to comply with the request of the Duke of Cea to compose a eulogy *en estilo culto* ("in the cultist style") *supra*, p. 28. In *Intrigue and Luck*, Jimeno, the *gracioso*, commenting on Blanca's apparent change of heart toward his master, Juan, criticizes the practice:

> With what a discreet style,
> with what sharp figures,
> with what new ambiguities
> she has known how to give you favors
> and make you jealous of Sol.
> With what terms so fitting,
> so short and true
> did she pursue the allegory
> of the moon, the sun and the sky.
> Not like some conceited person,
> in whose lowly verses
> there is a discord of allegories
> and confusion of conceits,
> plays on words,
> affectation and deception,
> foolishness to the ear
> and trickery of the faculties;
> for well observed, sir,
> it is music of instruments,
> which makes a sound and says nothing. (vv. 1248–67)

There is also a touch of ridicule in the speech of Lucía, maid to Blanca, in *The Test of Promises;* Lucía addresses her mistress not only in the sophisticated strophe of the *silva,* but in words hardly to be expected from a mere maid:

> Already I consider you "your excellency"
> and now on the rich dais
> surrounded by columns of silver,
> I behold your presence
> with such rare beauty
> that they may judge your greater fortune insufficient.

Now in the covered [sedan] chair,
happy shell of such a precious pearl,
I behold you accompanied by the retinue,
serving nobly and working leisurely,
of a hundred gentlemen
who obtain gifts (*dones*) only in their titles (*don*).

(*Ya te juzgo excelencia,*
y ya en el rico estrado,
de colunas de plata rodeado,
contemplo tu presencia
con tan rara hermosura,
que juzguen corta tu mayor ventura.
Ya en la cubierta silla,
concha feliz de perla tan preciosa,
te miro acompañar de la cuadrilla
noble sirviendo, y trabajando ociosa,
de cien gentiles hombres,
que sólo alcanzan dones en los nombres.) (vv. 1263–74)

Although he seems to be burlesquing the practice, Alarcón did
engage (and very effectively) in the art on occasion, particularly
in his two best-known plays. In a series of *liras,* Don Mendo of
The Walls Have Ears addresses Doña Ana in an unusually extravagant manner and in one strophe juxtaposes the journey of Doña
Ana in her coach from Madrid to Alcalá, the rape of Europa by
Jupiter, who in the form of a bull snatched her up and swam with
her on his back across the sea, and the voyages of ships bearing
their treasure from the Indies to Spain. The coach is a "Jupiter"
bearing another Europa; it is also a ship carrying *its* treasure
(Ana) from its Indies (the Manzanares, the river of Madrid), to
its Spain (the Henares, the river of Alcalá) (vv. 414–69).

In *The Truth Suspect,* the entire description of the fictitious
banquet on the banks of the Manzanares, some forty-eight verses,
is one long series of conceits: The embroidered figures are so real
as to lack only souls to be alive; the arrival of his lady causes the
stars to be envious and the grass to become emeralds, the sands,
pearls, and the water, crystal; the amount of ice used for cooling
the drinks is so great that the nearby Manzanares thinks that it is
again flowing through snowcapped mountains, and the festivities
end because Apollo is so jealous that he hurries the coming of the
day. It is, as his listener, Don Juan, says, depicted in such perfect

colors that one would not exchange hearing it for having been there (vv. 665–748). Alarcón did not abuse the practice and showed that he could be competent and clever at it when he chose.

IV   Alarcón and Characterization

Alarcón is frequently cited as the creator of the comedy of character. Arthur L. Owen writes[7] that "he studies his characters with conscientious thoroughness and a realistic psychology unique in the theater of his century," adding that *The Truth Suspect* and *The Walls Have Ears* are the best comedies of the period and that Don García of the former and Don Mendo of the latter are "universal types," which in a sense they are, the one glorying in tall stories and the other in belittling.

The study of characterization in the *comedia* is an elusive one:

The generic characteristic of the Spanish drama is, of course, the fact that it is essentially a drama of action and not of characterization. It does not set out to portray rounded and complete characters, though certain plays may do so incidentally. . . . We must . . . accept the fact . . . that the Spanish drama works on the assumption—which after all has the authority of Aristotle behind it—that the plot and not the characters is the primary thing. . . . This does not mean that the characters are unimportant. What it does mean is that since the dramatists are out to present, within a strict limitation of time, an action that is full of incident, they generally have not time to elaborate their characters, and must confine their characterization to brief touches.[8]

In spite of those who believe that Alarcón was interested solely in characters and used intrigue only as far as was necessary,[9] he was very much concerned with intrigue as all of his plays attest. The characterization evolves from the action and is secondary to it. Generally, Alarcón's men emerge more distinctly than his women. Basically, his *galanes* resemble those of Lope and Tirso, handsome, brave, concerned with their honor, possessed of the attributes of a gentleman, such as loyalty, trustworthiness as a friend, and chivalry, and usually hopelessly in love, but there are some notable differences as well, and one might say that as a group they are more intrepid and inventive than those of most of his famous contemporaries. They tend also to determine the direction of the play to a greater extent than the *dama* or *gracioso*, which is frequently the case in the *comedias* of intrigue of Lope, Tirso, or Calderón.

The *gracioso* was, perhaps, the most fascinating character of the *comedia*. He is more complex and paradoxical than the *galán, dama,* or *viejo* (father) and interests for what he says as well as what he does. It is not easy to define a *gracioso,* who could range from a merely comic figure in a minor part to the full-fledged character so denominated in the cast, who was at once the servant and companion of the *galán* and who played an important and lengthy comic role. In some of his characteristics, gluttony, buffoonery, cowardice, astuteness, impudence, and fondness for wine, he is founded on tradition and convention, which go back to the classic theater, but he also possessed certain characteristics which may have been observable in the servants of the time: inquisitiveness, loquaciousness, common sense, superstition, timidity in face of real danger, but impertinence when physical harm was not threatening.

Efforts have been made to differentiate the *gracioso* of Alarcón from those of other dramatists. Ermilo Abreu Gómez thinks that they are inhibited, lacking in wit, and modeled on the Indian servants of Mexico, and that their actions vacillate "between Indian timidity, Creole resentment, and Spanish boldness"; others have commented on the more serious attitude of the *gracioso* and the fact that he is more companion than servant.[10] Of the twenty authentic plays, eighteen have a character designated as the *gracioso* in the cast of characters, or *reparto,* which, presumably, Alarcón himself provided. Of these, only five are further identified: one is a servant, one a student, one a *villano,* and two are Jews, one of these being further designated a shepherd. The remaining thirteen serve in the capacity of servants to one of the *galanes,* although not always the leading *galán.* In *The Unlucky Feigner* and *Friendship Punished,* there is no *gracioso* so called in the cast, but in the former, Sancho, servant of the leading *galán,* has a *gracioso* role, and in the latter, it is Turpín, the servant of the old Dion. In addition, there are servants of other *galanes* who possess *gracioso* characteristics in that they are amusing. Even limiting oneself to the eighteen *graciosos* so called by Alarcón, there is a wide range in the manner in which they are presented and the parts that they play. Coridón (*Master of the Stars*) appears only as a peasant who has lost his wife to a secondary character. Campana, on the other hand, of *The Entanglements of a Deception*, precipitates the entire plot development because of his well-meaning blunders. The two best-known *graciosos* are Tristán of *The Truth Suspect* and Beltrán (*The Walls Have Ears*), who are, indeed, more serious, and serve as sober and learned counselors and companions to their respective masters, although not without a quiet, dignified brand of humor, but they do not contribute materially to the development of the plot.

The *gracioso* was useful as the mouthpiece of the author himself. Since he was permitted in the *comedia* to speak boldly and frankly to the highest personage, even the king, the author puts into his mouth ideas that could not be expressed appropriately by the other characters. How much was convention and how much Alarcón, cannot be said with certainty, but in a country and among people where hunting was a great sport, one must believe that Alarcón was talking for himself when he has Zaratán of *Cruelty for Honor's Sake* enter and say: "Oh! To the devil with hunting; for he undoubtedly invented it!" (*¡Ay! ¡Doy al diablo la caza; que él sin duda la inventó!*) (vv. 1–2) Why should he break a knee hunting when he could remain comfortably in Zaragoza? "What have the hares and the rabbits done to me?" (*¿Qué me han hecho/las liebres y los conejos?*), he asks (vv. 12–13). To the argument that hunting is practice for war, he replies that he would be no worse off to go to battle inexperienced than to die by drowning or from some other hazard while hunting.

Alarcón's ladies are generally of three types: the malicious schemer who loses out, the "good" schemer who triumphs, and a large number of rather colorless, shadowy women. For all of their excellent qualities, Doña Ana of *The Walls Have Ears*, Lucrecia and Jacinta of *The Truth Suspect*, and Doña Blanca of *The Test of Promises*, to mention the ladies of Alarcón's three best plays, never rise to being much more than pawns. Several of his *damas* give great promise of being spirited and independent, with a mind of their own, but the promise is usually short-lived. Miss Mireles Malpica attributes Alarcón's inability to create feminine characters to his "not having the experience in the matter of women that Lope had, nor does he know them as thoroughly as did Tirso de Molina." Miss Melvin, admitting that they lack the warmth of Lope's and the aggressiveness of Tirso's (and of Calderón's, she might have added), believes that they are individual with Alarcón, that nowhere else do we find a lady who has so much to say about her destiny, and who is usually the incarnation of discretion and good breeding, with a mind of her own.[11] She does not really have as much to say about her destiny as Miss Melvin implies, not as much as some Tirsian and Calderonian heroines, nor is she always an example of discretion and good breeding.

V Alarcón and the "Honor" Theme

When Lope de Vega, in 1609, wrote that, as a theme, "matters of honor are the best, because they move everybody powerfully," he was probably reflecting a practice more than recommending a procedure, for there is scarcely a *comedia* in which honor is not introduced in one form or another, sometimes humorously and sometimes gruesomely. Sometimes it was the main theme and sometimes merely incidental: "After [Lope's] time almost every writer of *comedias* seems to have felt compelled to make some references to the subject, even if it was not always used as a major motive in his works, as in fact it often was." [12] Thus Alarcón, as he imitated Lope and his contemporaries in other ways, also incorporated the honor theme and recognized its dramatic possibilities. He treated it comically and incidentally, as in *The Unlucky Feigner, The Resembler of Himself,* and *Everything Is Chance,* and seriously as the chief motivation, in *The Weaver of Segovia* and *Cruelty for the Sake of Honor.*

Lack of space precludes a discussion of the code of honor, its many, often subtle, ramifications, its relationship with Christian teaching, its reflection or condemnation of aspects of contemporary life, its equation (or lack thereof) with virtue, or the perennial argument between *honra* (honor earned or bestowed) and *honor* (honor inherent or innate). The honor code of the *comedia* is much more rigid than was the case in real life and became strictly a convention, as much desired and expected as the use of the *gracioso*, intrigue, and other elements that make up the *comedia:*

. . . the code of honour in the Spanish drama of the Golden Age is a convention which, although not entirely divorced from reality or from morals, is closely concerned wih neither of these things, and a defence of the code of honour, or an attack on it, should not refer to the conditions of real life, nor to any contemporary moral opinions, without bearing in mind that it is bound up with the popular entertainment of the time. One might suggest also that the makers of popular entertainment may not always have accepted without reservation the conventions upon which their productions were often based.[18]

Although Alarcón was not as preoccupied with "honor" as some of his contemporaries,[14] there is no play in which he does not introduce it in some way. For the most part, the remarks and actions of his characters follow the conventional, from clichés (such as that the loss of honor is worse than death itself or that like glass, the slightest breath [of scandal] will cloud it, or that once broken it cannot be restored) to bloody vengeance; in one of his last plays, *Cruelty for the Sake of Honor* (vv. 2155–58), "honor" asks "love" for pardon since "the offense dies only in vengeance" (*sólo muere el agravio en la venganza*). Nevertheless, he does give the theme some unusual twists, which are more for dramatic effect than a dissent from convention or indignation at the rigidity of the code.

Efforts have been made to show that Alarcón differs from his contemporaries in his attitude toward the code. The observations of Barja have already been noted (*supra,* p. 39) and A. A. van Beysterveldt states that in Alarcón's approach to the code, there is a "tendency to despoil honor of the excessive radiance with which it is generally surrounded in the theater of his time," adding that it is colored with idealism and commenting on Alarcón's "moderation in vengeance" and his "laudable intention of humanizing social norms." [15] But such restraint in vengeance is absent in *Everything Is Chance,* in which an anonymous and rash *galán* pays with his life for making advances to the supposed lady of his slayer; in *The Weaver of Segovia,* where another Don Fernando forces the violator of his sister to marry her and then kills him in a duel; or in *Master of the Stars,* in which Licurgo not only slays Teón, who had slapped him when he was the peasant Lacón, but does so in a rather underhanded manner. In *Intrigue and Luck,* Arnesto, the unscrupulous rival and enemy of Don Juan, falls from his horse and is hurt. Juan hastens to his aid and boldly tells him that

> it is honorable valor
> to give strength to a rival
> in order to kill him later;

for it is no great deed
to be victor over one ailing.

(*es honrosa valentía
dar fuerza al competidor
para matarlo después;
que de un doliente no es
hazaña ser vencedor.*) (vv. 1591–95)

The distinction between an "honorable man" and a "man of
honor," with the shallow conception of the latter, is very well illus-
trated in a scene from *The Weaver of Segovia,* in which the Marquis Suero Peláez, having caused the execution of a man and the
ruin of his family by false accusations, tells his son in a model of
advice that not by inheritance, but by exemplary conduct is one a
gentleman and worthy of esteem; what really bothers the old man
is that his son threatens to bring disgrace on the family by getting
involved in a brawl with a man "worth so much less than you,"
because of a "lowly" woman. Neither the marquis nor his son considers himself anything but a man of honor.

Alarcón has been cited as one author of *comedias* who believed
that nobility of conduct was more important than nobility of
birth, and there are, in fact, two excellent passages in support of
this claim: the scene from *The Weaver of Segovia* (vv. 558–629),
just mentioned, and vv. 1416–19 of *The Truth Suspect.* Notwithstanding them, however, is the fact that all of Alarcón's better
characters are of good birth, although the *galanes* are sometimes
poor and complain that being of a noble heritage is given scant
consideration in a materialistic world. In this connection, it is sin-
gular that from his pen we have no play that exalts the concept of
honor among the more lowly, such as we find in plays of Lope,
Calderón, or Vélez de Guevara. In *Master of the Stars,* Teón, a
courtier, runs off with the wife of Coridón, a peasant, and Alarcón
makes the cheated husband a pathetically ineffectual man with
regard to his honor, and the butt of some pointed jokes by his
companions.[16] There is nothing in Alarcón's theater to support the
belief that his opinions of the conventional honor code differed
from those of his contemporaries. He saw the dramatic possibilities of the honor theme and used it to good effect, even to the
point of giving it an unusual turn on occasion: In *Master of the*

Stars and *Cruelty for the Sake of Honor,* it is the offended husbands who die, the first a suicide, the second a victim of murder, as the resolution of the problem of lost honor.

VI   *The Theme of Loyalty*

A second theme and yet a concomitant of the honor code in the *comedia,* is that of loyalty to one's lord, mainly to one's king. There are no fewer than six kings in Alarcón's plays, including one fictitious King of Crete and the impostor, Nuño Aulaga, and one queen regnant, as well as two heirs apparent, Prince Enrique of Trastamara, and a "Prince of Bohemia." Alarcón's characters are neatly divided into those, the good ones, who are unswervingly obedient and respectful to their lords and those, the bad ones, who are not. Even those admirable characters who do not approve of their monarch's escapades may remonstrate and suggest, but they do not rebel. Alarcón may have had two reasons for the abjection with which his characters treated the royal person, one the convention, already established, that the king's person was sacred and his word law, and only God was to judge him; the theory of the divine right of kings was firmly rooted. The other was that he was still seeking a position on one of the king's councils and it would not be diplomatic to suggest other than complete loyalty.

It was not uncommon in the *comedia* to picture the king or his heir as a rather scurvy fellow, but in the end each redeems himself by renunciation of his illicit passion, repentance of his actions, restoration of a fallen favorite, or a similar laudable act. Professor Carlos Ortigoza believes that in his plays, both serious and jocose, Alarcón is protesting against the Spanish king and that he treats him as stupid, myopic, and of little moral substance, thus making fun of him, something that Lope would not permit to such an extent.[17] It is true that his kings are not on the whole very admirable. When his role is that of a *galán,* the Alarconian king or prince is no worse, if no better, than Lope's assortment of royal characters. Where the king is a dispenser of justice, rather than a *galán* (*How to Win Friends; The Weaver of Segovia*), he assumes a more noble character. The lone queen, Petronilla (*Cruelty for the Sake of Honor*), is not the heroic figure that is Tirso's María de Molina, but she conducts herself with dignity.

Even more significant than the actions of these royal characters is the attitude of their subjects towards them. In *The Cave of Salamanca,* although the king does not appear, the mere mention of his name elicits such comments as making slaves of his subjects with "such human clemency," "who will not obey such a kind and holy king?" and "his holiness and prudence promised no less" than the leniency he showed to the magician Enrico. In *Everything Is Chance,* in which again the king is only mentioned, his pardoning the duke and the bailiff evokes the statement, "such a sentence from such an intelligence." In *Master of the Stars,* Licurgo is drawn out of the retirement he prefers because a king's will must be obeyed, and he replies that "the will of the king is a just law. I obey him" (vv. 457–59). Ricardo, of *Friendship Punished,* abandons his love for Aurora when he learns that the king also loves her (vv. 1488–91). Juan Encinas of *How to Win Friends* tells Don Diego that the word of kings is law and Diego replies that "there is no law, Encinas, to obligate a king, because he is the author of laws" (vv. 2226–28). One of the best examples of this exaggerated reverence is that of Don Juan of *The Favors of the World:* After he has been defeated and then spared by García and García, in turn, has been raised to a high position by the prince, Juan says that he, too, is honored since he who bested him is so honored. Undoubtedly more sincere, even though Alarcón was seeking royal favor at the time, are two references to Felipe III, reigning when *The Cave of Salamanca* and *The Truth Suspect* were written: In the former he is called a kindly and saintly king (v. 2703) and in the latter, a "saintly and perfect king" (v. 1782).

Nevertheless, Alarcón is, on occasion, mildly didactic. There is a tinge of sarcasm in *The Privileged Breasts* when Count Melendo, who has every reason to suspect the king of improper designs on his daughter, says:

> Pardon,
> King, if I have unjustly
> blamed your sacred person.
>   It was an error, not malice,
> to presume blame in a king
> who is the life of the law
> and the soul of justice.
> . . . You are the king,
> even though you do not seem so;
> but with me, merely to hear

> that you are is sufficient
> for me to drop my sword.
> And even though this offense,
> since I am as noble as you,
> could move this sword
> to avenge my dishonor,
> if the king must esteem his life
> less than his reputation as just,
> dropping it [the sword] now
> gives me greater vengeance;
> since the more offended the
> more loyal I appear,
> I avenge more since I prove you
> so much the more unjust. (vv. 766–72, 868–84)

His majesty remonstrates and Melendo adds that if he offended
the king in his words he would prefer returning them to his breast
to offending him (vv. 905–8). On still other occasions, courtiers
(Rodrigo in *The Privileged Breasts*, Filipo in *Friendship Punished*,
and Fadrique of *How to Win Friends*) point out to their respective sovereigns that their actions do not become a man who
is supposed to set an example for his people.

VII   Amistad *or Friendship*

Amistad, or friendship, is the third of the important motivations
of the *comedia,* but whereas an entire *comedia* may revolve
around the theme of honor or of love, or both, *amistad* is a more
incidental ingredient. Although "friendship" is the translation of
amistad, it is not an exact one, but a very restricted and special-
ized meaning because *amistad* is a bond between two men of
honor brought about by an action that either obligates the debtor
or requires a show of gratitude. It takes precedence over love, but
can be sorely tried when pitted against one's honor or loyalty.[18]
The obligations of friendship are great. In *The Resembler of Himself,* Ricardo, asking no questions or explanations, agrees to leave
his beloved and make the long and dangerous journey to Peru in
order to help out his friend, Juan, and in *How to Win Friends,* a
precious lesson in how to earn friends the hard way, Fadrique,
having given his word to protect a fleeing swordsman, must continue his protection even though he learns that the man whom he
has freed from the police and is harboring is the murderer of his

brother. Castro Leal (p. 147) states that each person in the latter play has good reason to operate for personal reasons, but do not "because friendship acquires for them the imperative character of an ethical norm." It is, then, not affection, but gratitude, duty, and obligation which determine "friendship." However, real friendship and loyalty are portrayed and Alarcón has given us some good examples in the characters of Garcerán of *The Weaver of Segovia,* Carlos and Fadrique of *Examination of Husbands,* and Ricardo, though a minor character, of *The Resembler of Himself.*

VIII   *Love as a Theme*

Paradoxically, love, although the last as a claim on the loyalties of a *galán,* is also the most important motivation. It is usually temporarily thwarted by the conflict of other loyalties throughout the *comedia* but emerges triumphant at the end and at no expense to the others. It is a concept of love strange to the present age. It is often love at first sight, almost wholly dependent upon physical attractiveness, but not completely independent of the knowledge that the *dama* is both wealthy and of good family. In *The Truth Suspect,* García, inquiring about the beautiful woman he has just seen, is told by Camino, her squire, that besides being beautiful and virtuous, "her father is a widower and old; two thousand ducats will be what she will inherit." García is overjoyed: "Do you hear that, Tristán?" Moreover, adds Camino, she is of a very good family. "Love," cries García, "I ask your wings for such a noble subject." Even the marquis of *Changing for the Better,* although he has fallen madly in love with Leonor and is not bothered by her poverty, takes a second look so as to be sure that she is of good family and honorable.

The *galán* often, it seems, would like to enjoy his lady without the bother of having to marry her, but this is unacceptable in polite society, and even when he succeeds in having an affair premaritally, he is forced either to pay with his life (*The Weaver of Segovia*) or to marry the girl (*Intrigue and Luck, The Unlucky Feigner*). Since marriage also brings with it a dowry and the wife's income, it has its compensations, and this prospect, together with the need of continuing the family name, makes the *galán* eager to get down to business. The *damas,* if anything, are even more precipitous in trying to bring about a consummation of the courtship than the *galán*. In the words of Jimeno, of *Intrigue and Luck:*

> By heavens,
> I think that you have forgotten
> how short life is for you
> in these times.
>   In the old days a man
> used to live five hundred years:
> if he took fifteen or twenty
> in courting and misunderstandings,
> it was not very much; but now
> that sixty is a great age,
> he is very foolish
> who woos for more than a month. (vv. 2359–70)

Rarely does Alarcón portray love in a sympathetic fashion, that is, as a genuine, sincere, self-sacrificing attraction. There are the peripatetic lovers such as kings and princes, those who, like the respective Ricardos of *The Resembler of Himself* and *Friendship Punished,* can give up a lady with no pangs, and those who marry someone other than the one they had in mind at the beginning of the play (*The Truth Suspect, Cruelty for the Sake of Honor*). The interest lies rather in intrigue than in emotion, in suspense rather than in decision, and in spite of the obstacles placed in the way of the so-called lovers, it is not so much that love triumphs as that respectability has been able to emerge from the entanglements that the author has woven. The object, especially on the part of the ladies, is matrimony and the solution is to give each a mate. But, whereas the emotion is cold and superficial, the intrigues are dramatically exciting, ingenious, and carefully worked out, and one can only hope that the quickly-matched, often mismatched, couples will have a happy wedded life.

IX   *Other Motivations*

Along with those already mentioned, there are two other motivations which usually accompany love and honor and which are nonexistent without them. One is *celos* and the other is vengeance. *Celos,* or jealousy, like *amistad,* has a broader meaning than the English word implies. It may mean jealousy or envy on the part of the *galán* or *dama,* who thinks that he, or she, has a rival. It also involves "suspicion," when a character has reason to believe that his spouse or beloved has been unfaithful. It is, as Leonor says, in *Changing for the Better,* "smoke of the fire of love" (*humo del fuego de amor*), v. 164, but it may also arise where no love had formerly existed. Jealousy (*celos*) plays a role in almost every Alarconian *comedia,* from a particularly vicious one in *The Favors of the World* and *Intrigue and Luck,* in both of which it is instrumental in developing the plot, to a merely incidental or supporting one.

Alarcón gives us no play in which jealousy results in the wreaking of vengeance in such an extreme manner as in some of Calderón or Lope de Vega. The farthest that he goes is Fernando's slaying, in a duel, of the man who seduced his sister (*The Weaver of Segovia*); of the two dishonored husbands that he portrays, one dies by his own hand and the other by that of his supposed son. On the whole, seeking or exacting vengeance or satisfaction is incidental to the development of the plot; only some five men fall victim to the avenger's sword in the authentic plays: an anonymous *galán* of suspicious intent (*Everything Is Chance*) and Sancho (*How to Win Friends*), who die before the play is scarcely under way, and Teón of *Master of the Stars* and Juan and Suero Peláez of *The Weaver of Segovia,* who well deserved their fate. Otherwise, satisfaction is achieved through marriage or an explanation.

X   *Alarcón and the Classical Influence*

It was Juan Eugenio Hartzenbusch who, in the preliminary remarks to his edition (1852) of Alarcón's plays, wrote that Alarcón offered us more of a Terentian comedy than his contemporaries: "he is the classic of our theater." Menéndez y Pelayo in his history of Spanish-American poetry states that Alarcón's "principal glory" will always be that of having been the "classic" of a romantic theater. Henríquez Ureña(pp. 18–19) calls him an "artist of classical spirit," and comments on "his affinity . . . with the sober muse of Terence." From these remarks has come the oftenrepeated assertion that Alarcón is the "Spanish Terence," the "classical dramatist" among his contemporaries, a poet who protested against the theater of Lope.[19] The above statements, taken out of context, have tended to separate Alarcón's plays from those of his contemporaries more than was intended or is justified. Menéndez y Pelayo emphasized that he, Alarcón, did not break the formula of Lope's theater and Henríquez Ureña makes it clear that his designation of "classical spirit" was in the sense of a sober and reflective artist. Alarcón is a "classic" only in the meaning of a general perfection of his compositions, and even then, this reputation is based on but a few plays.

Alarcón undoubtedly read Latin; its study was part of the training of students, who (at Salamanca, at least) began with the grammar of Nebrija and continued through such classical writers as Plautus, Terence, Virgil, Horace, and Ovid.[20] He makes numerous classical allusions, both mythological and to Roman writers. Among the latter whom he names are Martial, Seneca, Terence, and Virgil. Millares Carlo notes a number of passages which he believes were influenced by classical writers, adding Cicero, Horace, Juvenal, and even Bias, one of the seven sages of Greece, to the above list.[21]

Although Alarcón makes no mention of Plautus, Eliza Pérez[22] maintains that he, even more than Terence, influenced the Mexican in similarity of structure, types, and ideas, but the similarity is tenuous at best and no greater in Alarcón than that between the work of his own contemporaries and that of the Roman poet. Alarcón's *comedia* is influenced solely by the standards set by Lope in construction, plot, and types, and where he differs in the development of characters, the apparent moral theme, and the more meticulous composition, it is owing rather to his own personality and training than to any direct classical influence.[23]

The mythological allusions are too numerous and too much a commonplace in the poetry, dramatic and lyric, of the *Siglo de Oro* to permit elaboration: Hercules, whom, as Alcides, he cites no fewer than four times as the symbol of strength; Antaeus, in the same sense; Argos, as the symbol of vigilance; Boreas, Eros, the Labyrinth of Crete, the River Lethe for forgetfulness, and Sinon, as an example of treachery. As with Alcides, he uses several of these a number of times (Lethe no fewer than seven, Sinon at least four). Such classical allusions were part of Spanish culture of the time, and do not imply an unusual or profound acquaintance with classical mythology.[24]

The unities, important in the classic theater, are not observed by Alarcón any more than by his contemporaries, and when they are it is more by accident than by design. That of action can be accepted only in the sense that the activities and affairs of all the characters pertain in some degree to the principal intrigue and, to be sure, in his better plays, *The Truth Suspect, The Walls Have Ears,* and *The Test of Promises,* the secondary elements are held in greater check than in the poorer ones. The unity of time is violently broken in Act I of *The Walls Have Ears* when a lapse of several days occurs within the act, contrary even to the advice of Lope (who also was indifferent to the unities) not to interrupt the limit or term of the day in an act. The unity of place is nowhere observed except that the entire action of some plays takes place within a given city (Sevilla, Madrid). The fact that there was no real reason to observe them did not prevent Lope from being rather apologetic, Tirso from appearing on the defensive, or some modern critics from trying to find a classical structure in Alarcón.[25]

In a general way, Alarcón's characters differ somewhat from those of his fellow playwrights: the *galán* is more aggressive, the *gracioso* less forward, the principal *dama* less intriguing, and the *viejo* less gullible, but, if anything, they are even farther removed from the characters of the Roman comedy, wherein the equivalent of the *galán* appears helpless, the servant is bold to the point of impudence, the lady is often a courtesan and rarely appears, and the "old man" can easily be taken in.

XI   *Alarcón as Moralist*

Even more insistently than the epithet "classical" or "the Spanish Terence," is that of "moralist" associated with Alarcón's name. Several studies concern themselves with the "moral" aspect of his plays. The late professor Mabel M. Harlan wrote that "in general Alarcón is designated as a moralist," and, combining the attributes of "classical" and "moral," César Barja declares:

When today we seek among the names of our writers of the seventeenth century that of a truly classical dramatist, we do not find that of [Lope, Tirso, or Calderón]. We find only that of Juan Ruiz de Alarcón. By classical we do not understand in this case what is usually understood, the opposite of romantic. No. We understand only the dramatist most perfect in form and most moral in thought. We understand the writer who is not of yesterday or of today, but who is of forever, . . . a writer who more than with the plot concerned himself with characters, a writer who punished vice and rewarded virtue, ...

Mirian V. Melvin, who expertly disposes of the myth of Alarcón's classicism, is not so penetrating with regard to the claim of "moralist": "Alarcón first set up his moral code, each vice and each virtue to be portrayed by a character, and around this he built his *comedia*." Ludwig Pfandl claims that he is "also the only one among the contemporary authors of the *comedia* who conceives the stage as a moralizing institution. His principal purpose is to unmask the defects of customs and to reward noble feelings." [26] This reputation as a "moralist" has been somewhat exaggerated. As James Fitzmaurice-Kelly says: "he has a high reputation as a moralist, especially among those who have not read *The Unlucky Feigner*" or, he might have added, *The Resembler of Himself*.[27] It is on *The Walls Have Ears* and *The Truth Suspect* that the reputation is based. The former is said to teach or show that slandering is wrong and the latter is a lesson in how lying does not pay, but this preoccupation with the "moral" aspect of the plays has obscured the skill with which Alarcón has used a human weakness to complicate plots which really begin with the usual tricks of the Golden Age drama, coincidence and eavesdropping in the first, mistaken identity and ambiguity in the second. A similar ironical twist is to be seen in both plays: whereas the respective *galanes* were otherwise intentionally, even maliciously, slandering and lying, they started their undoing unwittingly in a sincere, if misdirected, effort to further their love affairs. Only in *The Test of Promises* is it possible to make a case for a moral lesson: the exposure of ingratitude with the result that Don Juan loses everything, including the lady he was courting. But even of this work Castro Leal could write (p. 141) what is even more applicable to the others: "It is very easy to give to this *comedia* a moral sense, and, asserting that it condemns ingratitude, to put it beside *The Truth Suspect*, 'which condemns lying,' and *The Walls Have Ears*, 'which condemns slandering,' . . . But one can extract from a *cuento* or from a *comedia* a moral lesson on wisdom without either having been written precisely for that purpose." Again, in connection with *He Who Follows an Evil Way, Ends in an Evil Way*, Castro Leal writes (p. 82), that the play "has no moral purpose, even if its title tempts the uncautious to believe so. It was the custom of the time to baptize *comedias* with proverbs and adages without intending thereby to propose a thesis." In another study he blames the French, who knew only *The Truth Suspect,*

for the diffusion of the idea that Alarcón is a moralistic dramatist
and asks, "Is it true? Does Alarcón really set himself up as a judge
and dictate moral sayings?" He answers his own question: "Whoever reads his works without prejudgment will find that the case is
more complicated not only because the substance of a literary
work cannot be summed up in a moral, but because the ethical
consequences that could be deduced from his *comedias* are not as
evident as one is accustomed to believe." [28]

Although the so-called moral intent of Alarcón's plots is more
apparent than real, there are numerous verses which seem to
point a moral. Some of these bits of wisdom are conventional, not
peculiar to Alarcón, but they may well represent his own attitude:

> There is no worse enemy
> than he who wears the face of a friend
>   (or pretends to be a friend).
>
> (*No hay enemigo peor*
> *que el que trae rostro de amigo*)
>   (*The Favors of the World*, vv. 1846–47)

> The fabrication of one deception
> requires many deceptions.
>
> (*Muchos engaños requiere*
> *la fábrica de un engaño*)
>   (*Intrigue and Luck*, vv. 2205–06)

> As you sin, so will you pay,
> for he who commits the wrong
> will bear the punishment.
>
> (*Como pecas, pagarás,*
> *que él que la culpa comete,*
> *la pena quiere llevar.*)
>   (*The Resembler of Himself*, vv. 2158–60)

> There is a very long distance
> from saying to doing.
>
> (*Es muy larga la distancia*
> *desde el decir al hacer.*)
>   (*The Unlucky Feigner*, vv. 1755–56)

> Once a man begins to fall
> he never stops until reaching the last evil.

(*Si empieza a caer un hombre
hasta el postrer mal no para.*)
                    (*The Unlucky Feigner*, vv. 1311–12)

Since they say that the prison
is the touchstone of friends. . .

(*Pues dicen que la prisión
es toque de los amigos. . .*)
                    (*Everything is Chance*, vv. 327–28)

Let a man who thoughtlessly puts his sword
in the hands of a madman,
complain only of himself if,
when wounded [by him], he bleeds.

(*De sí mismo esté quejoso,
cuando vierta sangre herido,
quien la espada inadvertido
puso en manos del furioso.*)
                    (*Changing for the Better*, vv. 13–16)

The merchant seaman
with avaricious desire
each voyage that he undertakes
he says will be his last.

(*El mercader marinero
con la codicia avarienta,
cada viaje que intenta,
dice que será el postrero.*)
                    (*The Walls Have Ears*, vv. 117–20)

But according to what I think
no one will have a bad neighbor
if he himself does not give occasion.

(*Mas según lo que imagino
nadie tendrá mal vecino
si él mismo no ha ocasión.*)
                    (*Everything is Chance*, vv. 464–67)

XII *Alarcón and Mexico*

Much has been written about Alarcón's *mexicanismo* or *mexicanidad*, words difficult to translate exactly, but which refer to elements in his plays which some critics attribute to his birth in

Mexico and the influence of the early years spent in that country. Juan Pérez de Montalbán, a young contemporary of Alarcón but a devoted disciple of Lope, may have initiated this search for a "Mexican" quality in the man and his works in his compilation, *Para todos* (Madrid, 1632), wherein he refers to Alarcón's plays as having been put together with such novelty, cleverness, and "strangeness" (*extrañeza*) that there is no *comedia* of his that does not have much to be admired, words much different from those of 1623 when he compared the *mal formado* (ill-formed) *Descriptive Panegyric* with the twisted body of its supposed author. Quevedo is said to have had Alarcón's Mexican heritage in mind when he referred to him as *mosca y zalamero* (obsequious).[29]

The more notable students of Alarcón of the nineteenth century, Hartzenbusch, Fernández-Guerra, Menéndez y Pelayo, do not make a point of his *mexicanidad,* but beginning with the twentieth century, the notion that it was his Mexican birth and boyhood that made his plays different from those of his contemporaries began to be propagated. José María Vigil wrote (1908) that his birth there in itself imprinted an indelible character on him and, having received the greater part of his literary education there, he could not change either his nationality or his fatherland merely by moving to the Peninsula. In a celebrated lecture given in December of 1913 and published the following year, Pedro Henríquez Ureña expressed the belief that some of Alarcón's plays were written before 1614 (that is, before his return to Spain for the second time) and may even have been performed in Mexico, and sought to prove (p. 185) that "the unusual and exquisite dramatist, belongs, rightfully, to the literature of Mexico and represents in a perfect manner the spirit of the Mexican people," although he later admitted (p. 195) that all the qualities of Alarcón that he describes are in part derived from his own genius, in part from his experience with life, and in part from his Mexican nationality and education.[30] Henríquez Ureña seems to have been concerned chiefly with justifying the inclusion of Alarcón as one of the great products of Mexican literature, but the idea of Alarcón's *mexicanidad* appealed. It was taken up by Luis G. Urbina, José Esquivel Pren, and Alfonso Reyes, who as late as 1957 wrote that in spite of the lack of allusions to Mexico in Alarcón's works, "the penetration of a certain moral and sentimental atmosphere is constant. Such atmosphere is Mexican." [31]

The argument was attacked by Ermilo Abreu Gómez and has been effectively demolished by Antonio Alatorre.[32] At the time of Alarcón's birth, only sixty years had passed since the fall of the Aztec empire, a period rather short for the formation of a pronounced Mexican character. More important, Alarcón seems purposely to have separated himself mentally as well as physically from his native land. He took great pride in his Spanish ancestry, adapted easily to life in Madrid, and seems to have expressed little, if any, interest in, or nostalgia for, Mexico.[33] Indeed, what is singularly surprising about his plays is that there is so little concern about his Mexican heritage, so few allusions to his experiences in the land of his birth and boyhood.[34]

It would seem that this lack of interest was mutual, for Mexico took no interest in him either. During the colonial period, large numbers of plays from Spain, including those of Lope, Calderón, and Moreto, were imported into Mexico but there is no record of any of Alarcón's having been performed or read. Contemporary references to his works are practically nonexistent. The only writer who is known to have mentioned them during the seventeenth century is Baltasar de Medina in a chronicle published in 1682, but although he lists the plays of Alarcón's first volume, he was more impressed that he was a contemporary of Quevedo.[35] In a theatrical season as late as 1805–1806, only one play of Alarcón was performed, *The Weaver of Segovia*. In view of its romantic nature, this might be expected, but at the same time, the works of Lope, Vélez, Montalbán, Moreto, Rojas, Calderón, and other contemporaries were being presented.[36] Performances of *The Walls Have Ears* in 1844 and of *The Truth Suspect* in 1868 did not meet with public favor. On September 22, 1875, the Spanish actor Enrique Guasp de Péris inaugurated a season at the Teatro Principal in the capital by reading a poem of Justo Sierra dedicated to Alarcón and promising the production of plays by Mexican authors, but, as Luis Reyes de la Maza wryly remarks, this tribute was followed by a Spanish comedy! In fact, no Alarcón play was given the entire season. Mexicans did not take a real interest in him as one of their own until the present century, when Alfonso Reyes and Pedro Henríquez Ureña began the crusade that culminated in the books, articles, and performances which appeared in the tercentenary of his death, 1939; even a street was named for him.[37]

XIII *Alarcón and the Fair Sex*

As far as is known, Alarcón never married, but of at least one affair of the heart there is evidence: his reference to an illegitimate daughter for whom he provided in his will. The name of the mother was Doña Ángela de Cervantes, about whom nothing else is known. Professor Ruth Lee Kennedy has brought together and commented on numerous passages in works of his contemporaries that appear to make fun of the hunchback as a gallant.[38] She accounts for three women, one "it would seem, not only beautiful but of some social standing," another "lovely but completely mercenary," and a third "to whom there clings the fragrance, now faint, now intense, of academic circles," but their identity has eluded scholars to this day; one of them may even have been the mother of his daughter. The possibility that Doña Ángela (in spite of her title) was his housekeeper (*ama de llaves*) or even a "village girl of Cuenca" (*aldeana de Cuenca*) has been suggested by Castro Leal (p. 52). Except for his will, all that is known of this aspect of his private life is based on comment, caricature, and conjecture, but, Miss Kennedy writes, how much truth lies behind it "it is difficult to say, so heavily have the colors been laid on by his contemporaries," and concludes that in spite of a repelling appearance, he did find favor with women and was attracted to them and that this is both attested and explicable.[39] Alarcón, himself, in *The Walls Have Ears* (vv. 23–28) refers to incidents in which women became enamored of deformed men, and perhaps his attitude toward women may be seen in his plays. Some of his female characters are among the most disagreeable in the *comedia de capa y espada* (cloak and sword plays). Such notorious women as Jezebel and Semiramis, wicked women of plays of his contemporaries, are recreations rather than original concepts, but Alarcón's are the results of his own brush. Some are unprincipled, some emerge rather weak in character, still others are indistinct in portrayal. Few are warm human beings.

If, then, his *comedias* are a key, Alarcón's opinion of women was not of the highest. In *The Resembler of Himself*, the *gracioso*, Sancho, presents a new list of the seven wonders of the world, the first of which is a woman who is not always asking for something (*una mujer que no pide*, v. 16). They are "thieving harpies" (*arpías rapantes*) or they talk too much. Jimeno, in *Intrigue and*

Luck (vv. 1333–36), implies that they prefer to talk with strangers since it involves more freedom and less risk. They are vain, "for what will a woman not do to be called 'your excellency'?" (*que por llamarse excelencia,/ ¿qué no hará una mujer?*); they are changeable, for "he who tests a woman gives indications of being a fool," and "he is a fool who expects stability in a woman or in the sea." [40] The most frequent comments, and usually by the *gracioso*, are directed to their avarice and their loquaciousness. In an amusing scene of *The Resembler of Himself*, Sancho, a servant, tells his girlfriend that he is leaving for the New World. Her immediate reaction is to ask him what will he send her. He replies in mock reproach:

> Behold with what sorrow she receives
> the sad news of my absence! . . .
> Such is the tyranny
> of this infamous species
> that the echo of "I am coming" is "give me"
> and the echo of "I am leaving" is "send."
> Is there no "welcome" to the "I am coming"?
> Is there no "return quickly" to the "I am leaving"?
> (vv. 642–43, 646–51)

Inés shrugs her shoulders and retorts: "How silly! You tie up your purse strings and yet ask me to be true" (vv. 681–82).

Criticizing the greed, garrulousness, fickleness, and coquettishness of women, however, is a commonplace in the *comedia*, and Alarcón may merely have been catering to public taste in these remarks of his *graciosos*. More unusual and, therefore, perhaps more sincere is one of the nicest tributes (in *Everything is Chance*) to women to be found in Alarcón or elsewhere, and spoken by a *gracioso* at that:

> Madame, although I do not profess
> the formalities of a *galán*,
> there reigns in my heart
> no other thing than woman,
> there is no possession, in my opinion,
> more worthy of esteem.
> What spring adorned
> with fountains, plants and flowers,

what divine splendors
of the sun in its fourth sphere,
    what purple dawning,
what heaven full of stars
can equal the beautiful elements
of the face of a woman?
    What joy in illness;
in health, what contentment,
what solace in torment
can there be without her presence? (vv. 2231–48)

He continues with rhetorical questions referring to their inconstancy, love of money, being either easy of virtue or cold, each of which he answers in their favor, adding that if they are difficult to "get," men dislike it, if they are "easy," men do not esteem them.

An interesting sidelight to Alarcón's portrayal and criticism of women, is the frequency in his plays of scenes of violence or attempted violence against her person. In *The Walls Have Ears*, Don Mendo attempts to force himself upon Doña Ana after he has her coach driven off the highway. Only the greatest physical effort saves Doña Clara from the advances of Don Diego in *The Cave of Salamanca*, Leonor of *Everything Is Chance* avoids forcible possession by the duke, abetted by her "friend" and her servant, only by dashing around the room until help arrives. The noble "weaver" of Segovia forces his way into the house of a wealthy lady for the single purpose of stealing her jewels. Twice (*Friendship Punished* and *Master of the Stars*) a lady must threaten to kill herself to avoid the intended rape by an impassioned monarch. In *The Resembler of Himself* and *The Unlucky Feigner*, imposters, who have entered the house as cousin and brother, respectively, of the *dama*, go beyond the bounds of propriety in such relationships in their advances toward the ladies. Although in none of these plays do the *galanes* succeed in their nefarious designs, the Antichrist, in the play of this name, a different type of play, certainly, slays both his mother and the woman who has resisted him.

XIV   *Alarcón and His Faith*

In view of the elaborate provisions that he made for the repose of his soul, Alarcón's faith must have been a firm and unquestioning one and in his works there is nothing to contradict this, but the Christian religion plays only a small part in his production. He wrote only one play with a definitely religious theme, *The Antichrist*, but this displays an "almost negative attitude in the religious feeling of the period." [41] *The Stratagem at Melilla* has religious elements, but like *The Antichrist*, is mechanical and devoid of deep, religious feeling. The same mechanical reaction is to be observed in the episode, already discussed (*supra*, p. 39), of the *Favors of the World*. Don García, of *The Cave of Salamanca*, who has taken refuge from the law in a church, remarks that although Christian, he is getting a little tired of having to remain in his sanctuary (vv. 2338–42), and in *The Resembler of Himself* (vv. 2128–54), Sancho has some unkind comments for women and their devoutness, declaring that they would become Moors if it meant more money, that they appear devout so as to avoid being burned at the stake, that they go to mass only to be seen by the *galanes*, and that when they recite the rosary the beads (*cuentas*) are a means of keeping an account (*cuentas* also) of what they intend to do a man for, as much a criticism of women as of religious hypocrisy.

Alice M. Pollin suggests that for Alarcón reason and intelligence must be humanly or divinely directed, that these with knowledge are always acknowledged to be gifts of God. She also thinks that he was "deeply concerned with the spectral images of Luther, Calvin, and other possible threats to his faith." [42] He appears to have accepted without question the teachings of the Roman Catholic Church, to have followed the formalistic practices conscientiously, but to have exhibited little interest beyond this.

XV *Magic, the Supernatural, and Astrology*

As for many, the occult held a certain fascination for Alarcón, and he makes use of it, in one way or another, in four of his twenty authentic plays. He was very careful, however, to go on record as not according any support to its practices or beliefs. In *The Test of Promises*, which in a sense is not a play of magic at all since it requires no exhibition of magical or supernatural trickery on stage, Don Illán, the magician, himself says that although he knows the art, "To practice black magic is wrong, but I never saw anyone punished for knowing it" (vv. 569–72). In *The Cave of Salamanca*, Enrico, the magician, loses a debate in which it is "proven" that of the three types of magic, black magic, alone, being the work of the devil, is sinful. The perpetrator of sinful magic in *The Antichrist* goes to perdition but "good" magical works are considered divinely inspired, both in this play and in *The Stratagem at Melilla.*

Augusta M. Espantosa-Foley has studied the antecedents of the opinions regarding the occult and its use in Spanish literature prior to Alarcón as well as by Alarcón himself.[43] She believes (pp. 124, 150) that Alarcón, in his plays, first established his orthodoxy with regard to the Church's doctrine and that he then felt free to employ it for its dramatic effect. He did not "preach" against it (p. 100), but he recognized its theatrical nature and "regarded the occult arts as a means to an end in the creation of a dramatic work" (p. 150). Although she devotes the major portion of her study to *He Who Follows an Evil Way Ends in an Evil Way,* of less than certain attribution, her conclusions apply even more forcefully to the authentic works.

Astrology also interested Alarcón, an interest he shared with other dramatists of the day.[44] On the surface there would appear to be a conflict between belief in the power of the stars and planets to control human destiny and that of the idea of the exercise of the free will as a part of Christian doctrine, but they, and he, managed to avoid any difficulty here in the thought, rather often expressed, that although the stars could influence ("incline") the will of men, they could not force it; thus they would indulge in the pleasant fantasy of astrological influence without appearing to question divine direction. Both the Marquis of Villena and Enrico of *The Cave of Salamanca* tell of studying this science, along with palmistry and black magic. The stars, the Ptolemaic system, the signs of the Zodiac all lent themselves to colorful imagery, and Alarcón uses astrological terms for comparison. In *The Truth Suspect,* the *gracioso,* Tristán, tells how he tried to learn his prospects, or future, at court, from the position or "aspects" of the king, often referred to as the sun, but with results as inconclusive as those of astrology.[45] Mention has already been made (*supra* p. 69) of the passage in the same play which compares various types of women with heavenly bodies. Astrology as a main element of a play, however, appears only in *Master of the Stars;* Licurgo's belief in the power of the stars is countered by the king's reply that he neither respects nor fears astrological predictions because he

has always thought them illusory (vv. 1160–63). Although
Licurgo thwarts the actual prediction of the stars, of killing a king
or being killed by one, there is a killing and it results from the
actions of a king. Nevertheless, Alarcón "chose the topics of astrology and fate not for the purpose of expounding theology but
rather to exploit their valuable dramatic possibilities." [46] It was the
theatrical, not the didactic, aspect that appealed to him.

XVI *Alarcón and the Concept of Free Will*

In conflict with the influence of the stars is the exercise of free
will (*libre albedrío*), the idea that man had the ability to make his
own choice, usually between salvation and damnation. The devil
could tempt and the stars could seek to influence, but neither
could control the will of one who did not wish it. The theological
concept is presented in *The Antichrist*, in which Sofía resists
every effort, human and diabolical, and retains her Christian faith
until martyrdom, but it is a concept applied also to love and virtue. Don Juan of *The Resembler of Himself* remarks that not even
the heavens (that is, the stars) themselves force a free will (vv.
1809–10), Doña Clara of *The Cave of Salamanca* warns Don
Diego that his magic cannot do so, "for sorcery has no hold upon
the free will" (vv. 1863–64), and Doña Ana of *The Walls Have
Ears* makes a similar remark about fate: "The inclination is of
heaven [again, the stars]; to consent or not is mine, for fate has no
jurisdiction over the will" (vv. 938–41). In *Friendship Punished*, a
play in a pagan setting, the free will appears about to be over-
powered. Both Policiano (vv. 105–8) and Filipo (vv. 701–4) seek
to justify their questionable activities by claiming a force greater
than the free will, and the king maintains that love is the effect of
the stars in which the free will has no part (vv. 1003–7), but it is
mere oratory; the free will never yields to the stars.

XVII *The Humor of Alarcón*

One does not think of Alarcón as a humorous playwright in the
manner of Lope de Vega or Tirso de Molina and, in fact, his is a
somewhat more subdued sense of humor, but he had one. Some of
his humor is forced. There are moments of slapstick, but usually
he is both gently amusing and pithily clever, as demonstrated not
only in individual remarks, but in episodes as well. Most of the
humor is to be found in the words and activities of the *gracioso*

and, therefore, extraneous to the plot, but the exchange between Sol and Nuño in *Intrigue and Luck,* and between Arseno and Celia in *The Unlucky Feigner* are excellent examples of subtlety and sarcasm. The reaction of those involved when Arseno, in the latter play, appears as a long-lost brother, not knowing that he has been preceded by another impostor, when in the same play and later in *The Truth Suspect,* a *galán* appears whole and sound after his supposed death has just been described in a gory fashion, and when Tello of *Everything Is Chance* learns that his expected misfortune has turned out to be the contrary, must be observed to be appreciated fully, but the reader can well imagine the pleasure of the audience.

Another type of humor is that found in the criticism of the foolishness and discomfort of ball playing (*The Walls Have Ears,* vv. 1059–77), bullfighting (*The Resembler of Himself,* vv. 1039–58), and hunting (*Cruelty for the Sake of Humor,* vv. 1–44), as well as in the *juegos de palabras* (plays on words), although, in this, he was not so successful as Tirso de Molina, or even Calderón. Already mentioned are *cuentas,* meaning both "beads of a rosary" and "accounts," and *don* meaning both a gift and the title "don." In *The Unlucky Feigner,* Celia asks the *gracioso,* Perea, what has happened to his master? Has he married? *No más que con dos esposas* ("only with two *esposas*") replies Perea (vv. 935–36): Arseno is in prison and although *esposa* means "wife," it also means "handcuffs." In *Changing for the Better,* Redondo, the *gracioso,* describing the Calle Mayor or "Main Street" of Madrid, remarks that it is a "street in which it is wise to be silent" (*calle en que es bien se calle,* v. 487). One pun impossible to translate, also found in *Changing for the Better* (v. 2332), is Redondo's remark: *No ves/que ya los hombres son hembros?,* in which *hembro* is a masculine form made up by Redondo on *hembra,* implying that men have become like women. In *The Resembler of Himself,* occur the verses:

> DON JUAN. *Sancho amigo, no convino . . .*
> SANCHO.   *¿Sancho, amigo, y no con-vino?*
> *Pues sin vino, ¿qué será?* (vv. 459–61)

Literally, Don Juan says, "Friend Sancho, it was not suitable," and Sancho replies, "Friend Sancho, and not with wine?/Well, without wine, what can it be?," in which "it was not suitable" (*no convino*) sounds like "not with wine" (*no con vino*), a horrid thought to Sancho and to the usual *gracioso*, who is pictured as a great tippler. A similar pun appears in *The Favors of the World* (vv. 833–34). The count (*conde*) refuses Hernando's request for alms and Hernando says to himself: *¿Este es conde? Sí; éste esconde/la calidad y el dinero* ("This is a count? Yes; this [one] hides [*esconde*] his nobility and money"). In *The Privileged Breasts*, Cuaresma (Lent), the servant of Ramiro, says that just because one must fast during Lent does not mean that Lent (that is, Cuaresma) should fast and he goes on to "prove" that eating will get one to heaven, since he who eats well, drinks well, and he who drinks well, sleeps well, and while one is sleeping he commits no sins (vv. 1392–1423).

Alarcón also introduces, on occasion, a *cuento* or tale, to illustrate a point. There are no fewer than ten in the authentic works, in every case told by a *gracioso*, and usually of a humorous nature, such as that of the Biscayan (*vizcaíno*) in *Everything Is Chance*, who aimed a gun at a neighbor and when the neighbor protested that he might kill him, replied that he would shoot him very gently (vv. 451–58), or that of two lovers who began their courtship quarreling and now continue squabbling so as not to break the habit (*The Resembler of Himself*, vv. 2103–18), or that of a coward who cried out that he had been killed by his adversary; when bystanders pointed out that he had not even been touched, he replied: "Could I not have been killed?" Finally, there are the commonplace targets of ridicule well known to the audience, such as the Manzanares: In *The Test of Promises*, Don Enrique makes fun of this river of Madrid, much maligned because of its lack of water, by saying that what little it has is merely perspiration caused by the heat.

XVIII *Alarcón, the Lawyer*

Alarcon's legal training, or his inclination toward the legal profession, is apparent in his works: the matter-of-fact versification, the straightforward plot, and the comparative lack of complication in development. It is further indicated in the effort of two characters, Licurgo in *Master of the Stars* and Zaratán in *Cruelty for the Sake of Honor*, to present to their respective monarchs laws which they think should be enacted for the good of the kingdom. If not altogether original with Alarcón, they probably reflect his views, and if Zaratán, like Sancho Panza, appears to speak lightly about such a matter as governing, the author himself is serious. His interest in logic and argument is apparent in the manner in which characters reason with each other or with themselves before deciding on a course of action, a device by which the audience is able to accept the plausibility of that action or development. Alarcón also introduces various legal terms and references. In *Intrigue and Luck* (v. 2558), the *gracioso* Jimeno refers to *primo oc[c]upanti* (the right of first occupancy), when he thinks that his master's *dama* is giving herself to the first man who comes along. In *The Cave of Salamanca,* he uses *mejorar* (v. 232) in the forensic sense of "to leave an additional bequest to someone," and *renunciaciones* (v. 995), "an allusion to the many and different clauses for waiving rights, which were stated in contracts of the time." [47]

XIX   Conclusion

Alarcón was an uneven playwright and the gamut of his production ranges from the very, very good plays to those that are extremely weak. In this he does not differ from his contemporaries, who, pressured for plays because of the popularity of the genre but short run of the works themselves, wrote many in great haste and with little thought. Alarcón's best known are *The Truth Suspect, The Test of Promises,* and *The Walls Have Ears.* Structurally and thematically, *The Test of Promises* is, for this writer, his masterpiece, but as a work for the theater and for broader appeal, *The Truth Suspect* is unsurpassed. Of more limited interest, but as well-constructed and excellent examples of the type of play that is the *comedia de capa y espada,* are *Everything Is Chance, Changing for the Better, The Resembler of Himself,* and *The Unlucky Feigner.* They are true comedies. At the very bottom of the list could be placed, in descending order, *The Cave of Salamanca, The Stratagem at Melilla,* and *The Antichrist.* The remaining plays can be ranked in between from the impressive heroic dramas such as *The Weaver of Segovia* to the unsuccessful efforts to recreate a pagan society (*Master of the Stars*). If Alarcón did write *It Is an Ill Wind That Blows no Good,* it must take a place among the very best of his compositions.

Alarcón's contributions to the *comedia,* to the Spanish stage, and to the theater in general are a carefully worked out plot, a minimum of extraneous activity, a direct and straightforward style, and a competent, correct, and ingratiating versification. In spite of his confession that he wrote only to tide himself over difficult times, it is apparent that he took pride and care in his craftsmanship.

The influence of Alarcón is difficult to assess. His plays did not achieve the popularity of those of some of his contemporaries,[48] and, in fact, the *comedia* of the Golden Age has had little impact upon world drama beyond furnishing plots to the French and English theaters and the vogue of Calderón, particularly in Germany. Very few *refundiciones,* or reworkings, of his plays were made in the years that followed his death, such as were made of the plays of Tirso, Lope, or Calderón. Leandro Fernández de Moratín (1760–1828) has been considered a successor in the Alarconian type of play and he certainly was acquainted with the *comedia,* but as has been pointed out, in order to return to that tradition, "Moratín followed a long ultrapyrenean detour, covering in reverse the road" that had been taken more deliberately by Corneille and Molière.[49] Alcalá-Zamora thought that the theater of Bretón de los Herreros (1796–1873), Ventura de la Vega (1807–1865), and even López de Ayala (1828–1879) to be closer to the type of Alarcón and that among the "patriarchs," Alarcón was the oldest and most influential on the modern comedy.[50] His influence, unfortunately, must be viewed through the composition and diffusion of *Le Menteur* and even though many (including Corneille himself) believe *The Truth Suspect* to be a superior work, it is unlikely that it or Alarcón would have achieved the reputation that each enjoys had Corneille not thought to imitate it.

When Lope de Vega died, in 1636, Alarcón was giving thought to returning to his native land, and an Italian, Fabio Franchi, published his *Essequie poetiche* or "Lament of the Italian muses at the death of *signor* Lope de Vega" (Venice, 1636)[51] in which he pleads with "His Majesty" (Apollo) to send a half dozen of his luminaries to seek out diligently Don Juan de Alarcón and "charge him not to forget Parnassus for America, nor ambrosia for chocolate, but that he write more *comedias* like that of *El mentiroso* and that of *Examen de maridos*" and refers to him as a learned craftsman *doctísimo artífice*), but Franchi's was a voice crying in the wilderness; Alarcón paid no heed. It is unfortunate, perhaps, that he did not yield to the plea of Franchi, but having written *The Truth Suspect* he must, if for this alone, be included among the great playwrights of Spain and the world's theater.

Notes and References

Preface

1. The full name and title of our author as he eventually came to sign himself was "El licenciado don Juan Ruiz de Alarcón y Mendoza." The degree of *licenciado* corresponds roughly to a master's degree and was granted to Alarcón in law. The title, *don,* is applied to the first name and was not assumed by Alarcón until after his return to Spain in 1613, although his mother had been addressed as Doña Leonor. The family name was Ruiz de Alarcón and his mother's maiden name was Mendoza. He is usually referred to, however, only as Alarcón.

2. As early as 1827, Pablo Mendíbal was placing him as one of the "great four." For a discussion of Alarcón's position in the hierarchy of Golden Age dramatists, see Alice H. Bushee, *Three Centuries of Tirso de Molina* (Philadelphia: University of Pennsylvania Press, 1939), pp. 50–53.

3. Earlier, but with less impact, Philarète Chasles, a French critic, had published in his *Études sur L'Espagne* (Paris: Amyot, Rue de la Paix, 1847) an enthusiastic, if somewhat misguided, laudation of Alarcón, and during the same decade, Alberto Lista was writing glowing accounts of Alarcón's plays (*Ensayos literarios* [Sevilla: Calvo-Rubio y Compañía, 1844], pp. 176–210).

4. Antonio Castro Leal, *Juan Ruiz de Alarcón, su vida y su obra* (México, 1943) pp. 17, 19. This, the best study of Alarcón, will be cited hereafter as "Castro Leal."

5. See *infra.* Chapter 2, note 1.

Chapter One

1. There is no record of either the date or the place of Alarcón's birth, but later documents support the assumption that, as suggested, he was born in 1581 or perhaps late 1580. A baptismal certificate once thought to be that of Alarcón and published in 1862 is not his, but of one Juan Ruiz [y Pérez], born in 1572. Alarcón himself invariably claims that he is a native of Mexico or of the city of Mexico of the province of New Spain, and Luis Fernández-Guerra y Orbe in

his biography, *Don Juan Ruiz de Alarcón y Mendoza* (Madrid, 1871), cited hereafter as Fernández-Guerra, writes succinctly (pp. 7–8): "He told us [that he was born in the city of Mexico] and repeated it without letup in all the documents of his career, in his verses, in the petitions as a jobseeker." Alarcón had at least one brother, Pedro, probably older, who, it is believed, was born about 1575. Alarcón himself mentions having *hermanos;* that is, at least two brothers or a brother and a sister. In the register of the University of Mexico, besides Pedro, three others with the name "Ruiz de Alarcón" matriculated during the last decade of the sixteenth century. They were Gaspar, born in Taxco (as was Pedro), Hernando, and García (since the place of birth of the last two is not given, can it be assumed that they were born in the city of Mexico?). For the marriage of Alarcón's parents, see Emilio Cotarelo y Mori, *Boletín de la Real Academia de la Historia,* II (Madrid, 1915), 525–26; for documents relating to his birthdate, Francisco Pérez Salazar, *Revista de Literatura Mexicana,* I (México, 1940), 155, and Francisco Rodríguez Marín, "Nuevos datos para la biografía del insigne dramaturgo don Juan Ruiz de Alarcón," *Unión Iberoamericana,* XXV (Madrid, 1911), 19; for the supposed baptismal certificate, *Boletín de la Sociedad Mexicana de Geografía y Estadística,* IX (México, 1862), 196; for his claim to Mexico as his birthplace, Dorothy Schons, "Apuntes y documentos nuevos para la biografía de Juan Ruiz de Alarcón y Mendoza," *Boletín de la Real Academia de la Historia,* XCV (Madrid, 1929), 114, and for the argument in support of Taxco, Julio Jiménez Rueda, *Juan Ruiz de Alarcón y su tiempo* (México, 1931), pp. 17–18 (see also Manuel Toussaint, *Taxco* [México, 1931], pp. 71–75); for his brothers, Schons, p. 66, and Nicolás Rangel, "Investigaciones bibliográficas," *Boletín de la Biblioteca Nacional de México,* X (México, 1913), 4–5. The studies of Rodríguez Marín, Schons, Jiménez Rueda, and Rangel will be cited by their names hereafter.

2. In his play, *Los favores del mundo* (*The Favors of the World*), Alarcón refers to the capture of Alarcón by Martínez de Ceballos and has as a character another historical person, Garci-Ruiz de Alarcón, so that he was aware of a relationship with this soldier, whose son, Rui Fernández de Alarcón, merited praise from Enrique III (Fernández-Guerra, p. 270).

3. According to Pedro de Ledesma, *Relación de las minas de Taxco* (composed in 1581, the probable year of Alarcón's birth, and cited by Castro Leal, pp. 212–22), the inhabitants had been moving out until only forty-seven miners remained. Fernández-Guerra, although at times more enthusiastic than correct, gives (pp. 1–7) further details about Alarcón's ancestry. For Alarcón's mother, see Castro Leal (p. 19), and for the family's connection with the mines of Taxco, see Schons (pp.

116, 133, 1ᴜ8, 141). A recent, very interesting and detailed study of the paternal side of Alarcón's family is that of Willard F. King, "La ascendencia paterna de Juan Ruiz de Alarcón y Mendoza," *Nueva Revista de Filología Hispánica*, XIX (1970), 49–86.

4. According to Rangel, a "Juan Ruiz, native of Mexico," matriculated in October, 1592, but it is not certain that this Juan Ruiz and Juan Ruiz de Alarcón were the same. See Rangel (X, 2, 7–8), also Pérez Salazar, p. 158. For an account of the university and the courses offered and degrees conferred, see Francisco de la Maza, *Las tesis impresas de la antigua Universidad de México* (México, 1944).

5. Gaspar received degrees in arts, canon law, and theology, and García matriculated in arts and canon law. Pedro received the licentiate in theology and became chaplain and rector of the Royal College of San Juan de Letrán. Hernando, a bachelor of theology and parish priest of Atenango, wrote a treatise about the superstitions and customs of the Indians of New Spain.

6. The relative was Gaspar Ruiz de Montoya, a prefect of the city of Sevilla. See Alfonso Reyes in the prologue to his edition of *La verdad sospechosa* and *Las paredes oyen*, *Clásicos Castellanos*, XXXVII (Madrid, 1948), vii–viii (cited hereafter as Reyes) and Rodríguez Marín (XXV, 3–4).

7. Fernández-Guerra, p. 19.

8. Aubrey F. G. Bell, *Luis de León* (Oxford, 1925), p. 73. Chapter III of this work is a good account in English of the University and the student life there.

9. In a petition of 1607, Alarcón states that he came to Spain to study at Salamanca "and for no other reason" (Rodríguez Marín, p. 19).

10. The fiesta is described in great detail in a letter which Fernández-Guerra believes (p. 34) was written shortly after the celebration by none other than Cervantes. The letter itself was reproduced by Aureliano Fernández-Guerra y Orbe in *Noticia de un precioso códice de la Biblioteca Colombina* (Madrid, 1864). From it, Fernández-Guerra assumed a friendship or an acquaintanceship between Alarcón and Cervantes, but neither Reyes (p. viii) nor Jiménez Rueda (p. 67) believes that Alarcón enjoyed the friendship of the author of *Don Quixote*. Professor Ruth L. Kennedy, "Contemporary satire against Ruiz de Alarcón as lover," *Hispanic Review*, XIII (1945), 164, believes the letter to be much later. There is no evidence that the two men were acquainted.

11. Fernández-Guerra, *Noticia*, p. 21.

12. Alarcón, like the other participants, had assumed a ridiculous name for the occasion, which Fernández-Guerra (pp. 41–42) explains as follows: "Finally Juan Ruiz de Alarcón, by virtue of being a florid

writer, because of being *flor y nata* (flower and cream) of the *pandos* or hunchbacked, because of his poor *talle* (figure) of a hunchback, and because of always being *de chunga* (in a jesting mood) and in good humor, and having been born in the Indies, took for himself the resounding, strange and meaningful name of Don Floripando Talludo, Prince of Chunga."

13. *Noticia*, pp. 29–30.

14. In a document of 1635 listing his services, he says that this occurred in 1607, and in a power of attorney granted on May 18, 1607, he states that he was already practicing before the *Audiencia* (Rodríguez Marín, p. 4).

15. Rodríguez Marín, pp. 18–20.

16. Schons, p. 113.

17. Rodríguez Marín, pp. 20–21; he adds that the other two were to travel in the capacity desired by Alarcón the year before, since in this way the expense of the voyage was reduced.

18. Alice H. Bushee, "The *Sucesos* of Mateo Alemán," *Revue Hispanique*, XXV (1911), 359–457.

19. De la Maza (cf. note 4 above), pp. 14–18, reproduces the thesis, plate 4. It consists of one page and only the conclusions are set forth. The argument is that the terms of a will are not binding if the beneficiary is not in a state (that is, dead) to accept them. See also Rangel, X, 11–12.

20. Rangel, XI, 8; Cristóbal B. de la Plaza y Jaén, *Crónica de la Real y Pontificia Universidad de México*, versión paleográfica de N. Rangel (México, 1931), I, 213.

21. De la Plaza, I, 219–20.

22. The document, now in the *Archivo de Indias* (Archives of the Indies) in Sevilla, is reproduced by Schons, pp. 140–41.

23. The document describing Alarcón's legal activities, also in the *Archivo de Indias* in Sevilla, is reproduced by Schons, pp. 140–41. To the excellent study of Miss Schons, I am indebted for many of the details concerning Alarcón's legal activities in Mexico. She also gives a good summary of what was involved in the duties of a *corregidor*. Rangel (XI, 60–62) reproduces some documents relating to García del Espinar.

24. See Jiménez Rueda, pp. 52, 89, 92, who cites the *constituciones* or rules of the university. Fernández-Guerra, p. 133, reported the existence of the autograph of the *vejamen* about 1816. See also Reyes, p. 267.

25. Rangel, XI, 23–24; La Plaza, I, 232–33.

26. Jiménez Rueda, p. 110.

27. All that is known of Pedro has been assembled by Miss Schons

in the study already cited. Her partial reproduction of this document takes up twenty printed pages. It is of interest in a study of Alarcón because it reveals in Pedro characteristics also noted in Juan: a desire for a position, a dissatisfaction with favors received, and an insistence upon his merits. Nevertheless, he seems to have been highly regarded in Mexico, as was the Alarcón family.

28. Dámaso Alonso, *Dos españoles del Siglo de Oro* (Madrid: Editorial Gredos, 1960), pp. 124–28. For the supposed insufficient remuneration, see Schons, p. 116.

29. Pérez Salazar, p. 160.

30. Jiménez Rueda, p. 110.

31. Juan Eugenio Hartzenbusch, in the prologue to his edition of Alarcón's plays, BAE, XX (Madrid: M. Rivadeneyra, 1852), xi. The prologue (pp. v–xii) is followed (pp. xiii–xxxvi) by a discussion of the characteristics of Alarcón's dramatic works.

32. See José Deleito y Piñuela, *Sólo Madrid es corte* (Madrid, 1942), pp. 23–24; and Karl Baedeker, *Spain and Portugal* (Leipzig, 1913), p. 60.

33. Schons, p. 87.

34. In 1615 he acknowledged receipt of twelve thousand *reales* in silver sent by Pedro. See Cristóbal Pérez Pastor, *Bibliografía madrileña o descripción de las obras impresas en Madrid*, III (Madrid, 1907), 465.

35. Hugo A. Rennert, *The Life of Lope de Vega* (Glasgow, 1904), p. 393; *Las paredes oyen*, vv. 1186–87. Rennert (p. 392) states that five hundred *reales* was the price and that Lope earned altogether about eighty thousand ducats from his plays. A rough calculation suggests that Alarcón received the equivalent of $1,000.00 for all of his, not including the income from publishing them.

36. See Carmelo Samonà, "Problemi ed aspetti della personalità di Alarcón," *Il Teatro di Juan Ruiz de Alarcón* (Roma: Tipografia Agostiana, 1953), pp. 40–41; Jiménez Rueda, p. 151; and Millares Carlo, I, xxix. In 1616, one Juan de Grajales, an actor and playwright, agreed to pay Alarcón five hundred *reales*, probably for a play, so that he had begun to compose for the stage by that year. We have no definite evidence of a composition of a play after 1626, when he finally received the position that he had been seeking. Alarcón was still trying to collect from Grajales in 1619.

37. For a description of the circumstances which brought about the composition of the play, see Fernández-Guerra, pp. 356–60, 502–3, and William A. Kincaid, "Life and works of Luis de Belmonte Bermúdez," *Revue Hispanique*, LXXIV (1928), 2, 11, 15, *et passim*.

38. Fernández-Guerra (pp. 386–87, 391–93) gives a lively account

of the genesis of the "Eulogy," or "panegyric," and includes the names of the collaborators. The *Elogio* (*Eulogy*), itself, is to be found in BAE, LII, 583–86, and in Millares Carlo, III, 393–407.

39. Fernández-Guerra (pp. 395, 508) attributes the *comentario* (commentary) to Quevedo. The *comentario* itself may be read in BAE, LII, 588–92 and in Millares Carlo, III, 407–18. Thirteen of these *décimas satíricas* "*a un poeta corcovado, que se valió de trabajos ajenos de varios ingenios*" ("to a hunchback poet who availed himself of others' efforts, by several wits") were published by José Alfay, *Poesías varias de grandes ingenios españoles* (*Varied Poems by Great Spanish Men of Talent*) in Zaragoza, 1654, and edited and reprinted by José M. Blecua in Zaragoza, 1946; in the latter edition they are to be found on pages 81–84. In Volume LII, 587–88, of BAE, Hartzenbusch published (1860) along with the *Eulogy* and the *comentario*, thirteen *décimas*, which differ in order and which substitute two different *décimas* for two in Alfay's collection. Except for Espina and Centeno, all of the contributors have a prominent place in any literary history of the period.

40. José Sánchez, *Academias literarias del Siglo de Oro*, (Madrid, 1961), pp. 53–54.

41. The episode is vividly described by Luis de Góngora in a letter to Hortensio Paravicino. The letter is quoted in R. Foulché-Delbosc, *Obras poéticas de Góngora*, Volume XXIV, Part 3, of *Biblioteca Hispánica* (New York: The Hispanic Society of America, 1921), 219, as well as in the *Obras completas* of Góngora edited by Juan and Isabel Millé y Giménez (Madrid: Aguilar, 1961), p. 1049. See the same editions, p. 18 and p. 552, respectively, for the sonnet attributed to Góngora which ridicules the timidity of the actor. See also Fernández-Guerra, pp. 290–92.

42. Fernández-Guerra, pp. 431, 522–23.

43. *Ibid.*, pp. 522–25.

44. Jiménez Rueda, p. 277.

45. Fernández-Guerra, p. 525, and Reyes, pp. 250–55.

46. *La verdad sospechosa* (*The Truth Suspect*) had already appeared in 1630, and *Examen de maridos* (*Examination of Husbands*) and *Ganar amigos* (*How to Win Friends*), in 1632, all under the name of Lope de Vega.

47. Schons, pp. 140–41.

48. Rennert, *Life of Lope de Vega*, p. 372.

49. It is not known where in the church Alarcón was buried. Joaquín de Entrambasaguas, *Estudios sobre Lope de Vega*, I (Madrid, 1946), 51, thinks it probable that it was in the chapel behind the high altar, but that at any rate, in one of the periodic removals of bones to make way for new burials, those of Lope and Alarcón dis-

appeared and the present resting place of whatever was mortal of Alarcón is unknown. See Rennert, pp. 372–73, and Entrambasaguas, pp. 38–54. In the newspaper, *A B C*, Madrid, May 30, 1968, it was announced that the probable coffin and remains of Lope de Vega had been discovered during an excavation in the church; for this information I am indebted to Professor John C. Dowling.

50. For the will, see Reyes, pp. 250–55.

51. Fernández-Guerra, p. 457.

52. The one in the cathedral at Taxco was made long after his death and does not agree with the descriptions of him. See Manual Toussaint, *Guía ilustrada de Taxco* (México, 1935), p. 20; and Reyes, p. xi. The idealized sketch which appears on the jacket, reproduced from Ferdández-Guerra, was originally an engraving by José Vallejo, based on the portrait in Taxco.

53. Reyes, pp. xi–xii; Carlos Vázquez Arjona, "Elementos autobiográficos e ideológicos en el teatro de Alarcón," *Revue Hispanique*, LXXIII (1928), 565; A. Valbuena Prat, *Historia del teatro español* (Barcelona, 1956), p. 190.

54. John C. Dowling, "Un envidioso del siglo XVII: Cristóbal Suárez de Figueroa," *Clavileño*, no. 22 (Madrid, 1953), 11–16.

55. In *Las paredes oyen* (*The Walls Have Ears*), he has a hunchback *galán* and in *La prueba de las promesas* (*The Test of Promises*) and *Examen de maridos* (*Examination of Husbands*) a *galán* is slandered by being falsely accused of having foul breath and other "defects." Also in *The Test of Promises* there are amusing references to the assumption of the title *don*.

56. Kennedy, pp. 145–65.

Chapter Two

1. Certain terms relating to the *comedia*, including those for the different strophes, are difficult to translate and will be retained in the original Spanish. These, besides *comedia* (except where it really means "comedy") are: *capa y espada*, which refers to contemporary drama of customs and was so called because the usual costume of the leading man included a sword and a cape; *dama*, the leading lady, or ladies; *galán*, the leading man or men; *gracioso* ("*amusing*") often the servant of the *galán* and the comic character of the play (his counterpart is a *graciosa*, usually maid to the *dama*); *viejo*, the father, uncle, or guardian of the *dama*. The strophic structure of the *comedia* is somewhat complex owing to the stanzaic variety used. Alarcón introduces some ten different types: Those employing the octosyllabic line are *romance* (of indefinite length, with assonance in the even lines; a similar strophe of six-syllable lines is called *romancillo*), *redondilla* (quatrain), *quintilla* (a five-line strophe of varied rhyme),

and *décima* (a ten-line strophe with a fixed rhyme scheme). Those strophes using hendecasyllabic lines, sometimes interspersed with heptasyllables, are: *octavas* (an eight-line stanza of fixed rhyme), *tercetos* (the *terza rima* of Dante), *lira* (a six-line stanza of varied line length and rhyme), *silva* (strophes of indefinite length and varied line length and rhyme), and blank verse (*versos sueltos*). Although in general each had a purpose, it was not rigidly dictated. For a detailed description of Alarcón's versification see S. G. Morley, "Studies in Spanish Dramatic Versification of the *Siglo de Oro*: Alarcón and Moreto," *University of California Publications in Modern Philology*, VII (1918), no. 3, 131–73, and Agustín Millares Carlo in his edition of Alarcón's plays, I, xxx–xliv. For a concise definition of the strophes, see Dorothy C. Clarke, "A Chronological Sketch of Castilian Versification Together with a List of its Metric Terms," *University of California Publications in Modern Philology*, XXXIV (1952), no. 3, 279–382.

2. For Hartzenbusch, see BAE, XX, xi. For other proposals of dates, see Fernández-Guerra, pp. 545–46 *et passim;* Castro Leal, p. 76 *et passim;* Pedro Henríquez Ureña, pp. 185–99; Alfonso Reyes, "Bibliografía de Ruiz de Alarcón," *Letras de México*, II (México, 1939), no. 8, 12. Bruerton's chronology appears in Volume I of Millares Carlo, xxix, and further references to it will be cited as Bruerton.

3. See the introduction of Professor Ebersole's edition of the first volume (*Primera parte de las obras completas*) of Alarcón's plays (Valencia, 1966), pp. viii–ix, and Ludwig Pfandl, *Historia de la literatura nacional española en la Edad de Oro* (translated from the German by Jorge Rubió Balaguer, Barcelona, 1952), pp. 461–62. Ebersole lists only the authentic plays. Pfandl includes only two plays in his last category, neither authentic.

4. Emilio Cotarelo y Mori, "Las comedias en los conventos de Madrid en el siglo XVII," *Revista de la Biblioteca, Archivo y Museo*, II (1925), 466–67.

5. Hartzenbusch (p. 509) offers 1448 as the date of action since in that year, the Prince, then twenty-three, became reconciled with his father, Juan II, after having fought against him. However, by then Garci-Ruiz would have been nearly eighty (Millares Carlo, I, 7).

6. Among them Castro Leal (p. 112); César Barja, *Libros y autores clásicos* (Brattleboro: The Vermont Printing Company, 1922), pp. 492–94; Manuel González de la Llana, *Teatro selecto* (Madrid: Tomás Alonso, 1868), p. xvii; Fernández-Guerra (p. 277).

7. Isaac Núñez de Arenas, in the Academy edition of Alarcón's works, II (Madrid, 1867), 349.

8. Castro Leal, p. 115, and Clotilde E. Quirarte, *Personajes de*

Juan Ruiz de Alarcón (México: El Libro Español, 1934), p. 91, respectively.

9. *Op. cit.,* p. 492. Barja continues: "His ethics and his religion were opposed to it. To conquer, yes; but after defeating the offender, it is greater nobility to pardon him than to kill him." Later, in *Ganar amigos,* the victor pardons his antagonist, who has fallen, because he admires his willingness to die rather than break his promise to a lady to keep a secret.

10. *Francisco de Rojas Zorrilla* (New York: Twayne Publishers, 1968), p. 121. MacCurdy comments that Rojas was "especially concerned with finding peaceful solutions to honor offenses."

11. Millares Carlo, I, 109, writes that the action is situated "in the fifteenth century, the time of Don Álvaro de Luna"; that is, the reign of Juan II, the same as the previous play, but this seems unlikely. The king mentioned in the play as the one born in Madrid is almost certainly Felipe III, born there in 1578. Juan II was born in Toro.

12. José Frutos Gómez de las Cortinas, in "La génesis de *Las paredes oyen,*" *Revista de Filología Española* XXXV (1951), 92–105, claims as a source a fable of Phaedrus, known and imitated during the Middle Ages, but there is little resemblance between the fable and the play. It has also been compared with Lope's *El premio del bien hablar* (*The Reward for Speaking Well* or *Opportunely*), but aside from the fact that Lope's *comedia* was written subsequently to *The Walls Have Ears,* its theme differs in that the *galán* wins his lady simply as the result of having said the right thing at the right time.

13. Castro Leal (p. 124) explains why he thinks that the Count of Villamediana could not have been the model. See J. P. Wickersham Crawford, *The Life and Works of Cristóbal Suárez de Figueroa* (Philadelphia: University of Pennsylvania, 1907), pp. 61–63, as well as Kennedy, pp. 145–49. Miss Kennedy adds (p. 148, n. 7) that for her it does not necessarily follow that the play is a direct answer to Suárez. Since it was performed on February 3, 1618, it was probably written in 1617.

14. In the introduction to his edition of *La verdad sospechosa* (Buenos Aires: Editorial Losada, 1939), p. 9.

15. For arguments for an earlier composition, see Castro Leal (p. 96), Henríquez Ureña (p. 9), and Fernández-Guerra (p. 172).

16. In 1615, Cervantes published a volume of plays which included one entitled *La cueva de Salamanca.* This clever little *entremés,* or farce, has nothing to do with Alarcón's play, magic, or the Cave of Salamanca, but is the account of the deception of a gullible cuckold by a student from Salamanca who pretends that he has learned magic in the famous cave.

17. See Samuel M. Waxman, "Chapters on Magic," *Revue Hispanique*, XXXVIII (1916), 325–463, an excellent and detailed account of the Cave of Salamanca and its legends, and of the life and legend of Enrique de Villena.

18. Herbert H. Bancroft, *History of Mexico*, III (San Francisco, 1883), 9 (pp. 7–11 give a good account of the construction of the *desagüe*). Martínez is also reported to have been born in Hamburg and in Mexico.

19. Waxman, p. 400. Later (but before 1645) Francisco de Rojas Zorrilla wrote *Lo que quería ver el marqués de Villena* (*What the Marquis of Villena Wanted to See*), also an attempt to vindicate Villena (MacCurdy, pp. 130–31).

20. Quirarte, *Personajes*, p. 79, and Carlos Ortigoza, *Los Móviles de la comedia* (México: Ciudad Universitaria, 1954), p. 133, respectively.

21. Vv. 283–88. Fernando de Zárate y Castronovo, a fairly successful playwright of the second half of the century, wrote a play, *Mudarse por mejorarse* (published in *Parte diez y nueve de comedias nuevas y escogidas de los mejores ingenios de España* or *Part 19 of New Comedias Chosen from the Best Talents of Spain*, 1663). Except for the title and the fact that the protagonist seeks to transfer his affections to a more desirable object, a not infrequent occurrence in the *comedia*, this work has nothing to do with that of Alarcón, although a sedan chair plays an important, if different, role in both plays.

22. The play has been compared with *Ventura te dé Dios, hijo, que el saber poco te basta* (*May God Give You Good Fortune, Son, for Knowing Little Suffices for You*) of Tirso de Molina, in which a young man of little intelligence rises in the world through a series of fortuitous circumstances. The play was not published until 1634, although Doña Blanca de los Ríos, in her edition of the *Complete Works* (*Obras completas*) of Tirso, I (Madrid, 1946), 1515, believes that it was written in 1615.

23. Alberto Lista, cited in Millares Carlo, I, 560.

24. Castro Leal, p. 85.

25. See BAE, XX, 519.

26. In 1679, there was published in Madrid a *refundición*, or reworking, of the play, with the title *Quien engaña más a quien* (*Who Deceives Whom More*). This reworking has been attributed to Alarcón himself. Fernández-Guerra (pp. 174–75) believes that it is his and states that "he sought then to unencumber and enliven the action, improve the characters, justify the events, and suppress obscenities." The action has been transferred to Milan, the long-absent brother is in Lima instead of Rome, and all of the characters, except Tristán and Inés, have been given new, more conventional, names.

The plot is virtually unchanged, even to the scene of the *romance*. Castro Leal ignores it completely in his study, but Morley (p. 133) includes it among the authentic plays and notes no variation from his usual metric practices, although a *refundición* could well be expected to follow the original, particularly one written almost entirely in octosyllables. T. Earle Hamilton (in a study of Alarcón's "epistolary practices," *Hispanic Review*, XVII [1949], 127) notes that in the third letter of the reworking, the original *redondillas* have been replaced by *versos de silva*, "distinctly at variance with Alarcón's usage." Reyes (p. 262) doubts that it is Alarcón's, while Millares Carlo (III, xii, n. 22) and Hartzenbusch (p. vii) do not believe it to be his. Inasmuch as the earliest extant version appeared forty years after Alarcón's death (it was published in Volume XLV of a collection of selected *comedias*, Madrid, 1679), it is unlikely that it is his.

Chapter Three

1. Fernández-Guerra, however, states (p. 318) that it offers situations and incidents similar to those told of Lope de Vega and the Duke of Sessa.

2. Manuel Bernardino García Suelto, in an *examen crítico* (critical study), first printed in 1829, but cited here from BAE, XX, 522.

3. The other plays are *La amistad castigada*, *La manganilla de Melilla*, *Los pechos privilegiados*, and *La crueldad por el honor*. Not included in this group are *Los favores del mundo* and *La cueva de Salamanca*, which are built around a historical person rather than an event.

4. See the Loeb Classical Library edition of Plutarch, I (London: William Heinemann, 1914), 205–303.

5. Volume VI of the Loeb Classical Library (London: William Heinemann, 1918) recounts the struggle in detail. The citation is found on page 65.

6. Juan de Mariana, *Historia general de España*, XV (Madrid: 1820), xl. Alarcón changes the spelling to "Vanegas."

7. Luis Cabrera de Córdoba, *Relaciones de las cosas sucedidas en la Corte de España desde 1599 hasta 1614* (Madrid, 1857), p. 80.

8. *Historia de la literatura española*, II (Barcelona, 1950), 469–70.

9. Dora Bacaicoa Arnaiz, *Notas hispano-marroquíes en dos comedias del Siglo de Oro* (Tetuán, 1955), p. 40.

10. Philarète Chasles, in his *Études sur L'Espagne* (Paris, 1847), p. 160, places it among Alarcón's very best pieces, adding that Pimienta is the best character of the play—an amazing evaluation. Ellen Claydon, in a recent book, *Juan Ruiz de Alarcón, Baroque Dramatist* (Valencia: Artes Gráficas Soler, 1970), places this play,

along with *The Cave of Salamanca* and *The Antichrist* "among Alarcón's finest" (p. 70), but I find her method of evaluation questionable and her conclusions, unconvincing.

11. Brooks, in "*La verdad sospechosa:* The Source and Purpose," *Hispania,* XV (1932), 243–52; Owen, in his edition of the play (Boston, 1928), pp. xviii–xix; Pérez, "Influencia de Plauto y Terencio en el teatro de Ruiz de Alarcón," *Hispania,* XI (1928), 131–49; Tyler, "A Possible Influence on *La verdad sospechosa?" Bulletin of the Comediantes,* XXII (1970), 6–7; Melvin, *Juan Ruiz de Alarcón, Classical and Spanish Influences* (Ann Arbor, 1942), p. 63. Miss Melvin's study is a good refutation of the exaggerated claims of classical influence on Alarcón. The *ejemplo* to which Professor Tyler refers (see the edition of John E. Keller [Madrid, 1961], p. 221), condemns lying as the worst of vices. The *ejemplo* of Juan Manuel is an allegory about a tree planted by Truth and Falsehood.

12. See Julio Cejador y Frauca, *Refranero castellano,* I (Madrid, 1928), 101, and III (1929), 33, and Francisco Rodríguez Marín, *Más de 21,000 refranes castellanos* (Madrid, 1926), p. 163.

13. *Muchos engaños requiere / el sustentar un engaño* ("Maintaining one deception requires many deceptions"), *The Unlucky Feigner* vv. 2568–69; *¡A qué de engaños se obligan / los que emprenden un engaño!* ("What deceptions obligate those who undertake one deception"), *The Resembler of Himself,* vv. 1779–80; *Tantos los empeños son / en que un engaño me ha puesto* ("So many [or how many] are the difficulties in which one deception has placed me"), *The Entanglements of a Deception,* vv. 949–50.

14. Owen, p. xviii. Castro Leal (p. 136) writes that "in the history of the Spanish theater and even of the European theater, it is the first battlefield on which the comedy of character triumphs over the comedy of intrigue."

15. Tristán gives an ingenious account of the various kinds of women to be found in the capital: the truly chaste are angels, and the others range from those (planets) with complacent husbands to those (comets) available for a single night. He declares that he prefers quiet women to all others and admits that when he sees another beautiful woman, he immediately forgets her predecessor (vv. 291–364, 569–73, 397–400).

16. Before Alarcón could publish his play, it appeared in a collection attributed to Lope de Vega (Zaragoza, 1630) as *El mentiroso* or *The Liar.* Because of this, Corneille at first believed the play to be Lope's, but later acknowledged his error.

17. For Corneille's comments, see *Examen,* in Ch. J. Marty-Laveaux, edition of Corneille's works, IV (Paris, 1862), 137–38. Molière is reported to have said that without *Le Menteur* he might not have written

Le Misanthrope (Émile Picot, *Bibliographie Cornélienne* [Paris: A. Fontaine, 1876], pp. 489–90).

18. Adrien Cart, in *Classiques Larousse* (Paris: Librairie Larousse, 1933), p. 9.

19. For *Il Bugiardo*, see Joseph S. Kennard, *Goldoni and the Venice of His Times* (New York: Macmillan, 1920), p. 340. For its translation into more than a dozen languages, including Turkish and Chinese, see Nicolà Mangini, *Bibliografia Goldoniana, 1908–1957* (Venice: Istituto per la Collaborazione Culturale, 1961). For the Spanish translation, *El embustero engañado* (*The Liar Deceived*), by Luis A. Moncín, see Paul P. Rogers, *Goldoni in Spain* (Oberlin [Ohio]: The Academy Press, 1941), p. 41.

20. However, later in Alarcón's own century (*ca.* 1656), the brothers José and Diego Figueroa y Córdoba wrote a pleasant *comedia, Mentir y mudarse a un tiempo* (*To Lie and Change at the Same Time*), certainly suggested by *The Truth Suspect*. With its disguises, hidings, and brother-sister relationships, it is Calderonesque in tenor, and its protagonist, something of a Don Juan and a more deliberate and unimaginative liar than García, actually gets to marry the girl of his choice.

21. Albert D. Sellstrom, in his unpublished dissertation, "*La verdad sospechosa* in the European Theater: Adaptations, Reworkings, Translations" (University of Texas, 1949), has traced a number of versions, as have Émile Picot, *op. cit.*, and Mary A. Belden, *The Dramatic Works of Samuel Foote* (New Haven: Yale University Press, 1929). For translations of *The Truth Suspect*, see my *Ensayo de una bibliografía de Juan Ruiz de Alarcón y Mendoza* (Valencia: Editorial Castalia, 1964), and its supplement, in *Hispanófila*, no. 27 (Valencia, 1966), 23–42.

22. Cejador y Frauca, *Refranero* . . . , I, 43.

23. *Op. cit.*, p. 71. See also *La prueba de las promesas, infra,* p. 78.

24. According to Fernández-Guerra (p. 235), it was presented before Queen Isabel, the French wife of Felipe III, in her chambers in October of 1621, but had been circulating for five years with approbation in the theaters of Spain. He bases the first statement on the *Libros de la Cámara* (Chamber Records) of the royal archives, but gives no source for the second. It appeared first under the name of Lope in a collection entitled *Parte veynte y qvatro [extravagante] de las comedias del Fénix de España Lope de Vega Carpio. Y las mejores qve hasta aora han salido* (*Volume 24 [Spurious] of the Comedias of the Phoenix of Spain, Lope de Vega Carpio, and the Best that Have Appeared Until Now*), Zaragoza, 1633, where it bears the title *Amor, pleito y desafío* (*Love, Dispute, and Chal-*

lenge). Lope wrote a play with this title, but it is entirely different in subject. Alarcón does not list it among those plays that he indignantly reclaims in the preface to his second volume, although he adds "and others."

25. In his *El teatro español, historia y antología* II (Madrid, 1942), 932, Federico C. Sainz de Robles states that reminiscences of this play are to be found in Victor Hugo's *Hernani*. He does not refer to anything specific, but presumably he is thinking of the scene in Act III in which Don Ruy Gómez de Silva, having admitted Hernani, disguised as a pilgrim, to his castle, hides and protects his guest from Carlos V when the emperor demands that he turn over the outlaw. So firmly rooted is this obligation of hospitality that Don Ruy Gómez permits Carlos to abduct his intended bride rather than go back on the obligation to protect a guest. The sacredness of a promise is also emphasized in the final act when Hernani, having agreed to give even his life to Gómez if needed to aid him, commits suicide at his demand. But the inviolability of the laws of hospitality and the binding of a promise extend to ancient times and although Hugo displays a close acquaintance with Spanish history and tradition, he need not have read *Ganar amigos* to compose *Hernani*.

26. See, for example, Pfandl, p. 413; Fernández-Guerra, p. 235; Castro Leal, p. 149.

27. Castro Leal, pp. 116–17. The work, which apparently is extremely rare, contains references to the Apocalypse, the *Summa Theologiae* of St. Thomas Aquinas, St. Paul's second epistle to the Thessalonians, and St. John's first and second epistles, to which Alarcón makes reference in the second act, scene vii, of the play.

28. Castro Leal, p. 116.

29. As will be observed, all of the signs and portents that accompany the Antichrist are completely opposite to those of Christ, from his incestuous birth on, and since Christ is represented by the Greek letters *chi* and *rho* (X and P), the Antichrist is represented by P without the X, or cross.

30. Several women of the name Sophia were martyred in the early days of the church, three at least by beheading, but it is not clear that Alarcón had any of these in mind. Since "Sophía" means "wisdom" in Greek, the attribute fits Alarcón's character, because she recognizes the Antichrist as an imposter.

31. For example, he makes the false Elijah a captain general with orders to conquer Egypt, Libya, and Ethiopia: "And he shall have power over the treasures of gold, and of silver, and all the precious things of Egypt; and he shall pass through Libya and Ethiopia" (Daniel XI, 43).

32. Joaquín Casalduero, "El gracioso de *El Anticristo*," *Nueva Revista de Filología Hispánica*, VIII (1954), 307–15.

33. In his edition of Calderón's *El mágico prodigioso* (*The Wondrous Magician*), *Clásicos Castellanos*, LXX (Madrid, 1953), lxviii; *Historia de la literatura española*, II (Barcelona, 1950), 469.

34. See his edition of Lope's dramatic works, III (Madrid: La Real Academia Española, 1893), lxxviii–lxxix.

35. Ed. Barry, in the introduction to his edition of *La verdad sospechosa* (fourth edition, Paris, n. d., p. xiv) writes that "1606 finds him [Alarcón] in Sevilla, in the society of Cervantes who, in spite of his fifty-nine years, was seeking out happy company. With him, he visits the celebrated prisons of the town, studies their organization, as well as the customs of the prisoners," and goes on to say that this experience served him in *The Weaver of Segovia*, which "offers, in several places, close analogies with the *entremés* (farce) of Cervantes, *The Prison of Sevilla*." There is no evidence that Alarcón knew Cervantes in Sevilla and the *entremés* itself has been attributed to Cervantes without good authority. It is, moreover, an "unfunny farce" about a thief who is being prepared for his execution but who is granted a reprieve at the last minute. "All that is said and done in it causes only horror" (E. Cotarelo y Mori, in *Nueva Biblioteca de Autores Españoles*, XVII [1911], lxviii). There is no relation between this "farce" and the play of Alarcón. That he had occasion to visit prisons while practicing law in Sevilla is possible, but the prison plays a very small part in the play.

36. *La mujer disfrazada de hombre* or "the woman disguised as a man" was a frequent and favorite character of the *comedia* of the Golden Age, although this is her only appearance in Alarcón.

37. In his translation of some of Alarcón's theater (Paris, 1865), p. 21.

38. Castro Leal (p. 167) says that it was a type which he never again touched, but as will be seen, *La crueldad por el honor* is on the same order.

39. Dorothy Schons, "Alarcón's reputation in Mexico," *Hispanic Review*, VIII (1940), 139–44; she finds no record of a play of his being performed before this date.

40. John A. Cook, *Neo-classic Drama in Spain* (Dallas, 1959) pp. 106, 525–26.

41. See Federico C. Sainz de Robles, in *El teatro español*, II (Madrid: Aguilar, 1942), 932, and Fernández-Guerra (pp. 354–55). Castro Leal (p. 170) believes that Schiller did not know Alarcón, but there are some interesting similarities in episodes in Schiller's play and some of Alarcón.

42. For the general theme of outlaws or bandits in the *comedia*, see A. A. Parker, "Santos y bandoleros en el teatro español del Siglo de Oro," *Arbor* (Madrid, 1949), pp. 395–416; for Fernando, see Alva V. Ebersole, "Pedro Alonso, un ejemplo del poder creativo de Juan Ruiz de Alarcón," in *Actas del segundo Congreso Internacional de Hispanistas* (Nijmegen, 1967), pp. 309–18.

43. Hartzenbusch (p. 545), who notes a number of discrepancies between the two; T. Earle Hamilton, in his study of epistolary practices (p. 128), who noted that the handling of letters was markedly different from that of authentic plays; and S. G. Morley, (p. 148) because some of the versification differs from Alarcón's practice.

44. Valbuena Prat, *Historia del teatro español* (p. 235), believes it to be Alarcón's although he admits that "the superiority of the second part is incontestable." The latest to insist on assigning the first part to Alarcón is J. A. van Praag ("Las partes primera y segunda de *El tejedor de Segovia*," in *Homenaje: Estudios de filología e historia literaria lusohispanas e iberoamericanas,* [The Hague, 1966] pp. 463–75), who discounts the discrepancies between the two as oversights of Alarcón and backs his contention not only of authorship, but of priority with a number of arguments. They are not as convincing as those denying its paternity to Alarcón.

45. In the preface to the second volume of his plays (Barcelona, 1634), Alarcón includes *The Weaver of Segovia* among those *comedias* which are known to have been published under Lope's name before Alarcón could see them to the press. If he is referring to a similarly pirated edition of *The Weaver of Segovia*, it has disappeared. For a reference to the possibility that he knew and resented the "first part," see Professor Mabel M. Harlan's edition (with John M. Hill) of *No hay mal que por bien no venga*, in *Cuatro Comedias* (New York: W. W. Norton and Co., 1941), p. 306.

46. In his edition of the play (New York, 1928, 1942), p. 116.

47. Juan de Mariana, *Historia de España*, BAE, XXX, 237.

48. Mariana, *loc. cit.*

49. *Supra*, note 16; Millares Carlo, II, 658.

50. Mariana, pp. 298, 302, 316–17, and Antonio Ramos-Oliveira, *Historia de España*, I (México, n. d.) 405–11.

51. *De gestrafte Kroonzught*, by Dirk P. Heynck, 1650.

52. In 1842, the author of *Don Álvaro*, Ángel de Saavedra, Duke of Rivas, imitated the Alarcón play in his *El crisol de la lealtad* (*The Crucible of Loyalty*). The Duke's play, in three acts and in verse, with its *gracioso* character, Berrio, is in the mold of the *comedia*, which indeed he calls it, but it is heavily tinged with Romanticism. It is somewhat tedious and lacking in direction, but owes much to

Alarcón's. The honor motivation is no longer present, the imposter (who bears the name of one of Alarcón's lesser characters) has no heart for the usurpation, but is urged on by an unscrupulous monk and dies a natural death in his cell after capture, the queen (who is never named) as well as one of her ladies (Isabel) is in love with Pedro (Alarcón's Sancho) and the play ends with his postponing his marriage to Isabel for a year so as to prove himself after the treason of his father (who is really his father) by fighting the Moors for a year.

53. In his edition of the play, a Ph.D. dissertation, University of Texas, 1965, pp. 47–53. Mesonero Romanos (BAE, XLV, viii) thought that Alarcón imitated *Galán, valiente, y discreto* (*Gallant, Valiant, and Discreet*) of Antonio Mira de Amescua, but the relationship lies only in the appraisal of suitors as prospective husbands and in the fact that the man who wins has been secretly favored all along. Mira's play is probably later than Alarcón's, but if either play suggested the idea of the other, the author, in each case, has used it in an independent manner.

54. After Alarcón's death, it was also attributed to Juan Pérez de Montalbán.

55. Millares Carlo, in his edition of the play, in the collection *Clásicos Castellanos,* CXLVI (Madrid, 1960), xviii, is among those who believe that Alarcón wrote both texts and that the second is a revision. This is true as well, he thinks, of *La verdad sospechosa* and *Ganar amigos,* plays also published first as Lope's. Anderson (pp. iii–iv) also believes the first edition to be entirely Alarcón's and uses it to correct errors in the authentic text.

56. In his edition in *Clásicos Castellanos,* pp. xvii–xviii.

57. Anderson (pp. 27–33) gives a summary of this criticism. The play was translated into German verse as *Das Ehemänner-Examen* (Berlin, 1925), and in 1923, Tomás Luceño Becerra made a *refundición* or adaptation, which Anderson (p. 7) describes thus: "Some seventy-eight percent of the lines of the *refundición* are taken unchanged from Alarcón, and another eleven percent are altered only slightly. Luceño has shortened the original of 3,009 lines to 2,060 lines. Some of his additions and changes result in scenes of slapstick comedy or in passages of questionable taste."

Chapter Four

1. Pp. 369–71 and 504, where he writes that "it is sufficient to read attentively half a dozen of Alarconian *comedias* and as many of Luis de Belmonte in order to deduce the paternity of [this] *comedia*."

2. P. 246, in John M. Hill's reimpression of it, in *Revue Hispanique*, LXXV (1929). The plot, which is not a very pleasant one, has its scene in Portugal during the reign of that country's Pedro el cruel (Peter the Cruel) some time after the tragic death of his paramour, Inés de Castro. Suspecting that a royal visitor from Poland is having an affair with the wife of one of his courtiers, absent in the Algarve, the king himself stands vigil at his home. When the young prince appears, he and supposedly Blanca, the wife, are slain and the bodies thrown into a pool. However, it turns out that Blanca is innocent and the slain woman is her cousin who has been so rash and indiscreet as to forge a letter from Blanca hoping thus to yield herself to the prince and require him to marry her.

3. In *Parte Quarenta i Vna De Comedias De Diferentes avtore* (*Volume 41 of Comedias of Different Authors*) (Zaragoza, 1646) although a private performance before Philip IV on November 9, 1634 is recorded by G. Cruzada Villaamil, "Teatro antiguo español," in *El Averiguador*, I (Madrid, 1871), 74.

4. Irrelevant, but pleasant reading, is Fernández-Guerra's description of the event, because the compassionate cardinal-archbishop pardoned all of the condemned and the people remained figuratively frigid "upon seeing the porters returning with the wood on their shoulders without its having served to scorch (*achicharrar*) a single heretic."

5. The life and the trial of Román Ramírez are discussed in some detail by Angel González Palencia, "Las fuentes de la comedia *Quien mal anda en mal acaba* de don Juan Ruiz de Alarcón," *Boletín de la Real Academia Española*, XVI (1929), 199–222, and XVII (1930), 247–74, and by Julio Caro Baroja, *Vidas mágicas e inquisición*, I (Madrid: Taurus, 1967), 309–28.

6. The story is a very amusing one, about a lady who, when she quarreled with her lover, tore his collar. Since the collar as well as his other clothes had been borrowed, the inconvenienced lender asked the lady, when she had occasion to quarrel with her boyfriend, please to do it when he was naked,

> for, when anger overcomes you
> and you attack him when he's dressed,
> remember you're attacking
> all the friends by him possessed.

> (*que, cuando la furia os viene,*
> *si vestido la embestía,*
> *haced cuento que reñía*
> *con cuantos amigos tiene.*)   (vv. 53–56)

7. Harlan, p. 187; Bonilla y San Martín (Madrid: Ruiz Hermanos, 1916), p. xiv.

8. Harlan, pp. 291–92, where she describes the *golilla* and its history; the quotation, from Zabaleta's *El día de fiesta por la mañana* (1654), is cited there.

9. Harlan (p. 306) believes that this refers to the appearance of the "first part" of *The Weaver of Segovia*. We do not know the date of the composition of the play, but far from being a plagiarism, it was attributed to Alarcón himself. He might have been annoyed with this unworthy accretion to his own efforts, but it can hardly be described as the assumption by some "crow" of Alarcón's "plumage."

10. This scene reminds one of two authentic plays, in which the *graciosos* remark, respectively, on the folly of knocking a ball about and the foolishness of enduring the inconvenience of hunting.

11. All of the poetry discussed here can be read conveniently in Volume III of Millares Carlo, pp. 384–423.

12. A. Millares Carlo, "Dos notas de bibliografía colonial mexicana," *Filosofía y Letras*, no. 7 (1942), 105–6.

13. Cristóbal Pérez Pastor, *Bibliografía madrileña o descripción de las obras impresas en Madrid*, II (Madrid, 1907), 399–400, where the *redondillas* are reproduced; also Fernández-Guerra, pp. 229–30, 508. For the *marqués*, see Aurelio Miró Quesada S., *El primer virrey-poeta en América (Don Juan de Mendoza y Luna, marqués de Montesclaros)*, Madrid: Editorial Gredos, 1962.

14. See Fernández-Guerra, pp. 446–47; the quotation, cited by him, is from a chronicler of the time. The bull's reaction to this great reward is unknown, but the people were ecstatic, and there resulted a eulogy to the King by over ninety *ingenios*, or "wits," from the Prince of Esquilache to the provincial notary Juan de Piña, collected in a book entitled *Anfiteatro de Felipe el Grande (Amphitheatre of Philip the Great)*, collected by José Pellicer de Tovar and published in Madrid later in the year or in 1632. Alarcón's sonnet describes the victory of the bull over the lion and the respectful manner in which it met its death at the hands of the King, who, Alarcón implies, was offended because the bull had not sufficiently venerated the king of beasts. For the second sonnet see Millares Carlo, III, 420–21. For the festival, see Alfonso Reyes, "Ruiz de Alarcón y las fiestas de Baltasar Carlos." *Revue Hispanique*, XXXVI (1916), 170–76.

15. Two satires against Quevedo have also been attributed to Alarcón, but the attribution is extremely questionable. See Luis Astrana Marín, *Obras completas* of Quevedo (Madrid: Aguilar, 1943), 39–41, 665, 757, 792, 978–79, 1055; Hartzenbusch, BAE,

XXIV, 587–88; Reyes, 265; and Millares Carlo, III, 421–22. For the assignment of the "false *Quixote*," to Alarcón, see Adolfo de Castro, "Un enigma literario," *La España Moderna*, I (Madrid, April 1889), 157–83, and for the rejection by M. Menéndez y Pelayo, "El Quijote de Avellaneda," in his *Obras completas, Edición Nacional*, VI (Santander, 1941), 287–302, 388–90.

Chapter Five

1. For a brief explanation of the strophes, see Chapter 2, note 1.

2. Bonilla y San Martín, p. xxiii.

3. Since no original manuscript of his seems to have survived and the printers of that time were often careless, it is not possible to tell whether the occasionally missing or defective verses are owing to his lapse or the printer's.

4. Pfandl, p. 460; Mérimée and Morley, *History of Spanish Literature* (New York: Henry Holt, 1930), p. 357; Henríquez Ureña, p. 13; Arthur L. Owen, "*La verdad sospechosa* in the editions of 1630 and 1634," *Hispania*, VIII (1925), 85, respectively.

5. See Caroline B. Bourland, "Of Men and Angels," in *Smith College Studies in Modern Languages*, XXI (Northampton, [Massachusetts], 1939–1940), 6–9.

6. BAE, XX, xvi. Lore Terracini, "Un motivo stilistico: L'Uso dell' iperbole galante in Alarcón," in *Il Teatro di Juan Ruiz de Alarcón* (Rome, 1952), p. 86, says that this "observation sins perhaps from optimism" and lists other examples of repetition.

7. In his edition of *La verdad sospechosa* (Boston: D. C. Heath, 1928), p. xviii; see also Castro Leal, p. 196.

8. A. A. Parker, "The Approach to the Spanish Drama of the Golden Age," in *Tulane Drama Review*, IV (1959–1960), 42–43.

9. Barja (p. 483): "It is also drama of character, not of intrigue; there is intrigue sufficient for the characters to move, function and speak, but the main thing is not the intrigue itself." Juan L. Alborg, *Historia de la literatura española*, II (Madrid: Editorial Gredos, S. A., 1967), 359–60: "Characters alone matter to Alarcón and, alongside them, those situations which permit him to interweave his abundant reflections; . . . Alarcón in fact wrote only comedies of character."

10. Abreu Gómez, "Los graciosos en el teatro de Ruiz de Alarcón," in *Investigaciones Lingüísticas*, III (México, 1935), 189–201. An excellent summary of the concept of the *gracioso*, the opinion of Hartzenbusch and the propagation of his definition and its refutation are to be found in "El gracioso de Juan Ruiz de Alarcón y el concepto de la figura del donaire tradicional" by Joseph H. Silverman (*Hispania*, XXXV [1952], 64–69).

11. Melvin, p. 51, and Guadalupe Mireles Malpica, *La significación de Balbuena, Alarcón y Altamirano dentro de la evolución de la cultura literaria mexicana* (México, 1954), p. 71.

12. C. A. Jones, "Honor in Spanish Golden-Age Drama: its Relation to Real Life and to Morals," *Bulletin of Hispanic Studies*, XXXV (1958), 207. In general it is serious when conjugal honor (that is, a married woman) is involved, and amusing when the *dama* is unmarried, perhaps because the marriage of the latter is possible and usual in the end and cancels all doubts and suspicions aroused during the play. There are exceptions, of course: Guillén de Castro's *Los mal casados de Valencia* (*The Ill-Matched Couples of Valencia*) makes light of conjugal honor, and in Calderón's *El alcalde de Zalamea* (*The Mayor of Zalamea*) a dishonored daughter is relegated to a convent. Lope's opinion may be found in *Arte nuevo de hacer comedias en este tiempo* (*New Way of Composing Comedias in These Times*), first published in Madrid, 1609. See BAE, XXXVIII, 230–32, and Hugo A. Rennert, *Life of Lope de Vega* (Glasgow, 1904), pp. 178–84.

13. Jones, p. 206. Professor Jones also notes the discrepancy between Lope's private life and the code of his characters.

14. Jones, p. 207.

15. *Répercussions du souci de la pureté de sang sur la conception de l'Honneur dans la "comedia nueva" espagnole* (Leiden: A. J. Brill, 1966), pp. 76–77.

16. Alarcón himself seems not to have been especially fond of life outside of the capital. There is no play, such as some among those of Lope and Calderón, in which the country or noncourt life is praised. The scenes are generally the streets or the houses of the affluent. There is a brief, but artificial, country scene in *Master of the Stars* and part of *The Weaver of Segovia* takes place in the Guadarrama Mountains, but the closest that he comes to praising the idyllic life is in *The Privileged Breasts*, in which there is a song which exalts country life and condemns the court (vv. 1175–83).

17. In his *Los móviles de la "comedia"*, pp. 58, 84, 89. Professor Ortigoza includes the king of the first part of *The Weaver of Segovia*.

18. "May God never wish that in me love should win over friendship" (*No quiera Dios que en mí venza / el amor a la amistad*, in *The Resembler of Himself*, vv. 885–86), and in *The Favors of the World* (vv. 2952–54), Julia seeks to get García on her side by asking him whether "it is better to preserve the friendship [of the king] than remedy his [own lost] honor" (*Mira si te está mejor / el conservar su amistad / que dar remedio a tu honor*).

19. Hartzenbusch, BAE, XX, xxv. For Menéndez y Pelayo, see the *Edición Nacional* of his complete works, XXVII (Santander,

1948), p. 58. Jiménez Rueda (pp. 42–43) believes that Terence, in particular, influenced the structure of his theater; Alfonso Reyes (p. xxxi): "The work of Alarcón represents a moderate protest against Lope" and although he wrote within the broad lines imposed by the master, "a general distrust of the usual conventions distinguishes him."

20. Aubrey F. G. Bell, *Luis de León* (pp. 65–66).

21. Millares Carlo, in the notes to his edition. Gabriel Méndez Plancarte, however, in his *Horacio en México* (México: Universidad Nacional, 1937) admits (p. 19) that Horace is never mentioned in Alarcón, "who was not a Horatian poet" (p. 11), but he does cite some passages "reminiscent" of the Latin odist. Alarcón's use of Plutarch as the basis of the plots of two plays has already been discussed (*supra* pp. 60, 62).

22. In her study, "Influencia de Plauto y Terencio en el teatro de Ruiz de Alarcón," *Hispania*, XI (1928), 131–49.

23. Melvin, who, after analyzing the works of Plautus, Terence, and Alarcón, concludes that neither "the careless gaiety, nor the amused and easy nonchalance of Plautus" (p. 23) nor the "images from Terence's highly polished reproductions of Menander" (p. 46) are to be found in Alarcón; "his is a seventeenth-century *comedia*, his characters are seventeenth-century Spaniards. . . . He follows the rules of the romantic theater of his time, even in his subjectivity; . . . [he] is deeply indebted to that great master Lope de Vega" (p. 106). "It is doubtful whether [he] consciously imitated the Latin Classic writers. His acquaintance with them was extensive, but he shows no direct borrowing" (p. 105).

24. Classical allusions in Alarcón's plays is the subject of an M.A. thesis at the University of Tennesee (1940) by Eva Bessie Veynar, which is summarized by Gerald E. Wade in *Bulletin of the Comediantes* X (1958) no. 2, 6–9. Miss Veynar included plays attributed to Alarcón and with these found 201 different allusions, among them the use of Fortuna twenty-two times. Professor Wade adds that "here [in Golden Age writers] is a complete body of knowledge, vast in its quantity, intricate in the complexity of mythological relationships" and he wonders how often they had to "thumb classical volumes to refresh their memories." That the poets of the time were well acquainted with classical mythology, in spite of occasional slips, is obvious from any reading of the *comedia*, but this knowledge, by Lope's and Alarcón's time, might well have "become merely conventional, little more than epithets" (Wade, p. 8), without the need of referring to classical writers.

25. For Lope, see H. J. Chaytor, *Dramatic Theory in Spain* (Cam-

bridge: The University Press, 1925), pp. 16–17, and for Tirso, *idem*, pp. 57–63.

26. Harlan, p. 184; Barja, p. 479; Melvin, p. 34; and Pfandl, p. 460. From a reading of all of the plays it can be fairly stated that Alarcón was not more concerned with character than with plot, he does not portray each vice and virtue by a character, nor did he first set up a moral code and then construct his *comedia*. Pfandl's statement that his principal purpose was that of unmasking the defects of customs and rewarding noble feelings, cannot, in my opinion, be supported by a reading of the plays. Among the studies of the moral aspect are those of José María Castro y Calvo, "El resentimiento de la moral en el teatro de D. Juan Ruiz de Alarcón," *Revista de Filología Española*, XXVI (1942), 282–97; Alfredo de la Guardia, "El teatro moral de Juan Ruiz de Alarcón," *La Nación* (Buenos Aires, July 30, 1939), p. 2; Ángel Valbuena Prat, "La moral de Alarcón," *Historia de la literatura española*, II (Barcelona: Editorial Gustavo Gili, 1950), 461–64; and a number of dissertations.

27. In his *A New History of Spanish Literature* (Oxford: Oxford University Press, 1926), p. 319, although he goes on to say that "he lends to the drama a moral significance which it had not possessed before, while at the same time he avoids preaching at his audience."

28. "Juan Ruiz de Alarcón y la moral," *Filosofía y Letras*, III (México, 1942), 74, 76. In the second part of the study he refutes the theory of Valbuena Prat and Castro y Calvo (*supra*, note 26), based on Max Scheler's *Resentment in the Moral*, that the moral aspect of Alarcón is owing to his resentment of his own poverty and deformity, believing that although he had good reason to be resentful, he rose above it. Alarcón makes reference to physical defects in *The Walls Have Ears*, *The Test of Promises*, and *Examination of Husbands*, but except for a little self-pity in the first, the defects are treated rather lightly, indeed humorously in the last two. Poverty seems to have bothered him more and his *galanes* complain of it on several occasions.

29. Montalbán's remark is frequently cited. This is from the study of Antonio Alatorre, "La mexicanidad de Ruiz de Alarcón," *Anuario de Letras*, VI (México, 1964), 169, taken in turn from Montalbán's edition of 1661 (Alcalá), p. 545. For Quevedo's remark, see BAE, XX, xxxii, and Mireles Malpica, p. 66; some idea of the extent to which the idea of *mexicanidad* has been carried can be gained from the following remarks in the last work: "His boyhood and his youth spent in New Spain must have left a profound effect. . . . His characters spend more time within the house than on the street. . . . On the other hand, courtesy was a peculiar quality of Mexican

society, for which reason Juan Ruiz de Alarcón makes his characters
excessively courteous. . ."

30. Menéndez y Pelayo wrote that if we did not know Alarcón's
native country, it would be impossible to guess it from his works
(*Historia de la poesía hispano-americana*, in the *Edición Nacional*,
XXVII, 57). For Vigil, see *Historia de la literatura mexicana* (México, 1908), p. 124.

31. Urbina, *La vida literaria de México* (Madrid, 1917), pp. 51–
52: ". . . it was New Spain that impressed a gentle character on
his poetry, that placed in souls created by him a tenderness more
sweet and melancholy than that expressed by other geniuses, a gentler courtesy and a more pronounced politeness in his *galanes*, and
a more amorous cleverness in his *damas*, characteristics all of the
criollo spirit, the Mexican life, the spiritual ambient, characteristics
that still persist in my country [México]"; Esquivel Pren, "El sello
mexicano de Juan Ruiz de Alarcón," in *El Nacional*, México, August
4, 1957; Reyes, in the introduction to the edition of Alarcón's plays
by Millares Carlo, I, xvii.

32. Abreu Gómez, "Juan Ruiz de Alarcón," in *Letras de México*,
II (1939), 10; Alatorre, "Breve historia de un problema: la mexicanidad de Ruiz de Alarcón," in *Antología M[exico] C[ity] C[ollege]*
(México, 1956), 27–45, and "Para la historia de un problema: La
mexicanidad de Ruiz de Alarcón," in *Anuario de Letras*, VI (México,
1964), 161–202; the last, an amplification of the second, gives a
concise summary of the development of the notion, the arguments
of those both pro and con, and his own conclusion: ". . . The thesis
of the *mexicanidad* of Alarcón should never have been established
and this not only for lack of a basis on which to support it" (p. 198).

33. In 1635, the year after the publication of the second volume
of his plays and possibly ten years after he ceased writing for the
stage, he petitioned to return to the New World, seeking a post
there. The reason is not clear; perhaps as Dorothy Schons implies
(p. 81), he felt his days were numbered and he wished to die in
his native land, for at least one brother was still living. Nothing
came of the petition, of course, and there is no other evidence that
he was either homesick for Mexico or disappointed that he did not
get to return.

34. In her article, "The Mexican Background of Alarcón," *Bulletin Hispanique*, XLVII (1941), 45–65, Dorothy Schons lists (p. 45)
what she believes to be allusions to his native land, but the gleanings
are few and indefinite. There is only one unmistakable reference to
Mexico and that is the lengthy description of the *desagüe* (see *supra*,
p. 48).

35. Dorothy Schons, "Alarcón's reputation in Mexico," *Hispanic Review*, VIII (1940), 139–44.

36. J. R. Spell, "The Theater in Mexico City, 1805–1806," *Hispanic Review*, I (1937), 55–65. Even *The Weaver of Segovia* had its difficulties. Barely eleven years before, Colonel Benovia y Zapata, who was also the arbitrator for the theater (*juez del teatro*), had recommended that the first and second parts of the drama "should be excluded because of its extravagance and passages which can lead to nothing else than infusing in the mind of the less learned ideas foreign to Good Order," a recommendation that was promptly accepted by the Viceroy, Count de Revilla-Gigedo. See Armando de María y Campos, "El virrey conde de Revilla-Gigedo prohibió las representaciones de *El tejedor de Segovia* de Juan Ruiz de Alarcón, en abril de 1794," in *Vida Universitaria*, no. 258 (February 26, 1956), 2, 10.

37. See Schons, "Alarcón's reputation," p. 144; de la Maza, *El teatro en México con Lerdo y Díaz* (México, 1963), p. 27. *El Universal* (México, August 5, 1939), pp. 1, 6, describes the ceremonies attending the dedication of the street.

38. "Contemporary satire against Ruiz de Alarcón as lover," *Hispanic Review*, XIII (1945), 145–65.

39. *Ibid.*, p. 165.

40. The citations not indicated are, respectively, *Changing for the Better*, v. 481; *The Truth Suspect*, v. 569; *The Walls Have Ears*, vv. 2541–42; and *The Resembler of Himself*, vv. 1407–08, 2099–2100.

41. Ángel Valbuena Prat, *Historia de la literatura española*, II (Barcelona: Editorial Gustavo Gili, 1937), 344.

42. "The religious motive in the plays of Juan Ruiz de Alarcón," *Hispanic Review*, XXIX (1961), 33–44. Alarcón makes several references to Calvin, but does not appear to be obsessed with any threat; in one instance there is a pun on Calvin and *calvo* (bald). In his one expression of religious fervor, the sonnet to the Christ of Prete, he is indignant over the destruction caused by Calvinists.

43. In her unpublished doctoral dissertation, "The Use of the Occult in the *Comedias* of Juan Ruiz de Alarcón," (University of Pennsylvania, 1962).

44. F. G. Halstead, "The Attitude of Lope de Vega Toward Astrology and Astronomy," *Hispanic Review*, VII (1939), 205–19, and "The Attitude of Tirso de Molina Toward Astrology," *Hispanic Review*, IX (1941), 417–39.

45. See Joseph H. Silverman, "Oí . . . astrología," in *Nueva Revista de Filología Hispánica*, V (1951), pp. 417–18.

46. Augusta M. Espantosa-Foley, "The Problem of Astrology and

its Use in Ruiz de Alarcón's *El dueño de las estrellas*," *Hispanic Review*, XXXII (1964), 11. In her article (pp. 1–11) the author gives a good analysis of the play from this point of view.

47. For a study of Alarcón and the law, see Niceto Alcalá-Zamora y Torres, *El derecho y sus colindancias en el teatro de don Juan Ruiz de Alarcón* (México: Imprenta Universitaria, 1949). For the use of legal terms and their explanations, see the notes to Millares Carlo, I, 953, *et passim*. See also B. B. Ashcom, "Three Notes on Alarcón's *Las paredes oyen*," *Hispanic Review*, XV (1947), 378–84.

48. One need only consult the studies of Irving A. Leonard to note the dearth of Alarcón's works. In a document of 1713, reproduced in his "A Shipment of *Comedias* to the Indies," *Hispanic Review*, II (1934), 39–50, there is not a single play by Alarcón among the fifty-four listed. Among the performances of the Coliseo Theater in Lima of the season 1790–1793, or of the 1790 season of the theater of the same name in Mexico, one looks in vain for a play by Alarcón (Leonard, in *Hispanic Review*, VIII [1940], 93–112, and XIX [1951], 104–20, respectively). J. R. Spell, "The Theater in Mexico City, 1805–1806," *Hispanic Review*, I (1933), 55–65, lists only *The Weaver of Segovia*. Dorothy Schons, "Alarcón's Reputation in Mexico," *Hispanic Review*, VIII (1940), 141–44, found no mention of Alarcón's name in any of the lists of books shipped to the colonies in the seventeenth century. Charlotte Lorenz, "Seventeenth-Century Plays in Madrid from 1808–1818," *Hispanic Review*, VI (1938), 324–31, compiled a list of seventeen performances of three plays, compared with 235 performances of seventeen of Lope, 223 of ten of Cañizares, 205 of twenty-one of Calderón, and thirteen and twelve, respectively, of one each of Cubillo and Mira. A similar compilation by Nicholson B. Adams, for the years 1820–1850, (*Hispanic Review*, IV [1936], 342–57) shows fifty-seven performances of five plays, compared with 541 of twenty-eight of Tirso, 458 of twenty-three of Lope, 273 of fourteen by Moreto, 113 of eight by Cañizares; even Belmonte is represented with 106 performances of a single play.

49. Alcalá-Zamora y Torres, p. 9.

50. *Loc. cit.*

51. See BAE, XX, xxxvii.

Selected Bibliography

Very little by or about Alarcón is available in English and considerations of space preclude a very lengthy listing here. For a more extensive bibliography of works by and about Alarcón, see Walter Poesse, *Ensayo de una bibliografía de Juan Ruiz de Alarcón y Mendoza* (Valencia: Editorial Castalia, 1964) and supplement, *Hispanófila*, number 27 (Valencia, 1966), 23–42. Although not the only bibliography and now out of date itself, it is the most recent and most nearly complete.

PRIMARY SOURCES

1. Collections of Plays (in order of publication dates)

Parte primera de las comedias de don Juan Ruiz de Alarcón y Mendoza (Madrid: Juan González, 1628). Published by Alarcón himself and projected as early as 1621, it contains eight plays: *Los favores del mundo, La industria y la suerte, Las paredes oyen, El semejante a sí mismo, La cueva de Salamanca, Mudarse por mejorarse, Todo es ventura, El desdichado en fingir.*

Parte segunda de las comedias del Licenciado Don Juan Ruiz de Alarcón y Mendoza (Barcelona: Sebastián de Cormellas, 1634). Also published by Alarcón, it contains the remaining twelve of his authentic plays: *Los empeños de un engaño, El dueño de las estrellas, La amistad castigada, La manganilla de Melilla, La verdad sospechosa, Ganar amigos, El Anticristo, El tejedor de Segovia, La prueba de las promesas, Los pechos privilegiados, La crueldad por el honor, Examen de maridos.*

HARTZENBUSCH, JUAN EUGENIO. *Comedias de Don Juan Ruiz de Alarcón y Mendoza*. Volume XX of the *Biblioteca de Autores Españoles* (Madrid: Imprenta y Estereotipía de M. Rivadeneyra, 1852 and several times since). In spite of the criticism leveled at Hartzenbusch for altering the texts at whim, these are remarkably faithful to the originals which, in truth, have many errors, and the collection remains to this day the only accessible one-volume edition of *all* the plays attributed to Alarcón. In

165

his edition, Hartzenbusch makes what is probably the first serious effort to evaluate the work of the dramatist and to give some account of his life.

ABREU GÓMEZ, ERMILO. *Teatro completo de don Juan Ruiz de Alarcón.* In *Colección Ramo de Oro* (México: Compañía General de Ediciones, 1951). Although lacking *Quien engaña más a quien* and the play written in collaboration, it is a convenient, well-printed edition, but without commentary.

MILLARES CARLO, AGUSTÍN. *Obras completas de Juan Ruiz de Alarcón.* Three volumes (Mexico: Fondo de Cultura Económica, 1957, 1959, 1968). A definitive edition of all of the plays, authentic and attributed, based on the *princeps,* with commentary, copious notes, an extensive study of their versification, variants, and some bibliography, attractively printed. The third volume contains, in addition to attributed plays, his occasional verse and a bibliography.

EBERSOLE, ALVA. *Primera parte de las obras completas de Juan Ruiz de Alarcón y Mendoza* (Valencia: Artes Gráficas Soler. Estudios de Hispanófila, 1966). *Segunda parte,* 1966. A reprinting of the plays of the two volumes of the *princeps,* preserving the orthography and typographical structure of the original. The edition is not annotated, and the verses are unnumbered.

2. Authentic Individual Plays (in order of publication)

The play written in collaboration, *Algunas hazañas de las muchas de don García Hurtado de Mendoza, Marqués de Cañete,* first appeared in a separate (*suelta*) edition (Madrid: Diego Flamenco, 1622).

Three of Alarcón's plays exist in editions which antedate those authorized by him:

La verdad sospechosa, in *Parte Veynte y dos [extravagante] de las comedias del Fenix de España Lope de Vega Carpio* (Zaragoza: Pedro Verges, 1630), folios 87–110.

Examen de maridos, in *Parte veynte y qvatro [extravagante] de las comedias del Fenix de España Lope de Vega Carpio* (Zaragoza: Diego Dormer, 1633), folios 41–62.

Ganar amigos, in the same volume, folios 201–18.

3. Attributed Plays (first known edition)

La culpa busca la pena, y el agravio la venganza, in *Parte Quarenta i Vna De Comedias De Diferentes avtores* (Zaragoza: En el Ospital Real, i General de nuestra Señora de Gracia, 1646), folios 139–70.

No hay mal que por bien no venga, in *Lavrel de comedias. Qvarta parte de diferentes avtores* (Madrid: En la Imprenta Real a costa de Diego de Balbuena, 1653), folios 73–94.

Quien engaña más a quien, in a separate (*suelta*) edition of the first half of the seventeenth century and again in *Comedias nvevas, escogidas de los meiores Ingenios de España. Parte qvarenta y cinco* (Madrid: En la Imprenta Imperial, por Joseph Fernando de Buendía, 1679), folios 381–418.

Quien mal anda en mal acaba, in a separate (*suelta*) edition (Sevilla: Francisco de Leefdael, n.d.).

Siempre ayuda la verdad, in *Segunda parte de las comedias del Maestro Tirso de Molina* (Madrid: En la Imprenta del Reino, 1635), folios 68–90. *Cautela contra cautela* and *El condenado per desconfiado,* attributed to him by some, are also in this volume.

El tejedor de Segovia, first part, in several seventeenth-century *sueltas* without date.

4. Selected Editions of Plays

There are several collections of selected plays and numerous editions of individual plays. Of the latter, the following are the most useful because of the commentary and notes, which are in English:

ANDERSON, CARL D. (ed.), *Examen de maridos,* unpublished dissertation of the University of Texas (Austin, 1965).

BOURLAND, CAROLINE B. (ed.), *Las paredes oyen* (New York: Henry Holt and Company, 1914, 1931).

OWEN, ARTHUR L. (ed.), *La verdad sospechosa* (Boston: D. C. Heath and Company, 1928).

REED, FRANK O., and EBERLING, FRANCES (eds.), *Comedia famosa de La prueba de las promesas* (New York: F. S. Crofts and Company, 1942, originally published in 1928).

HARLAN, MABEL M. (ed., with JOHN M. HILL), *No hay mal que por bien no venga,* in *Cuatro comedias* (New York: W. W. Norton and Company, Inc., 1941, 1956), pp. 179–323.

Only one play, *The Truth Suspect,* has been translated into English. There are two versions:

DEL TORO, JULIO, and FINNEY, ROBERT V., in *Poet Lore,* XXXVIII (Boston, 1927), 457–530, a more faithful translation than

RYAN, ROBERT C., in *Spanish Drama* (New York: Bantam Books, 1962), 135–89.

5. Documents

Almost all of the known documents pertaining to the life of Alarcón, few as they are, have been published in one place or another. What they are and where they may be found are conveniently listed in Alfonso Reyes (ed.), *Ruiz de Alarcón, teatro,* volume XXXVII of the collection *Clásicos Castellanos* (Madrid: La Lectura, 1918), 247–55, and Antonio Castro Leal, *Juan Ruiz de Alarcón, su vida y su obra* (México: Ediciones Cuadernos Americanos, 1943), 229–43.

SECONDARY SOURCES

1. Bibliographies

LA BARRERA Y LEIRADO, CAYETANO ALBERTO DE. *Catálogo bibliográfico del teatro antiguo español, desde sus orígenes hasta mediados del siglo xviii* (Madrid: M. Rivadeneyra, 1860). Facsimile editions (Madrid: Editorial Gredos, 1969, and London: Tamesis, 1969). Indispensable for any study of the *comedia*.

MCCREADY, WARREN T. *Bibliografía termática de estudios sobre el teatro español antiguo* (Toronto: University of Toronto Press, 1966). An exhaustive index of all articles and many books on the Spanish drama published between 1850 and 1950.

2. Biographies

FERNÁNDEZ-GUERRA Y ORBE, LUIS. *Don Juan Ruiz de Alarcón y Mendoza* (Madrid: Imprenta y Estereotipía de M. Rivadeneyra, 1871). A basic work, but one which must be used with caution.

JIMÉNEZ RUEDA, JULIO. *Juan Ruiz de Alarcón y su tiempo* (México: José Porrúa e hijos, 1939). More emphasis on Alarcón's "time" (*tiempo*) than on the poet himself.

CASTRO LEAL, ANTONIO. *Juan Ruiz de Alarcón, su vida y su obra* (México: Ediciones Cuadernos Americanos, 1943). The best study of Alarcón available in any language.

3. Histories of Literature

FITZMAURICE-KELLY, JAMES. *A New History of Spanish Literature* (Oxford: University of Oxford Press, 1926). An old, but respected, history.

MÉRIMÉE, ERNEST, and MORLEY, S. GRISWOLD. *A History of Spanish Literature* (New York: Henry Holt and Company, 1930). A good factual and (although brief) critical account of Spanish literary figures.

NORTHUP, GEORGE T. *An Introduction to Spanish Literature.* Third edition, revised and enlarged by Nicholson B. Adams (Chicago: University of Chicago Press, 1960). A concise history of Spanish Literature in English.

4. The *Comedia*

CHAYTOR, H. J. *Dramatic Theory in Spain* (Cambridge: The University Press, 1925). A convenient collection of the dramatic ideas of the playwrights before, and contemporary with, Alarcón.

PARKER, A. A. "The Approach to the Spanish Drama of the Golden Age," in *Tulane Drama Review*, IV (1959–1960), 42–59. Originally printed in London: The Hispanic and Luso-Brazilian Councils, 1957. An excellent summary of what the *comedia* is and intended.

REICHENBERGER, ARNOLD G. "The Uniqueness of the *Comedia*," in *Hispanic Review*, XXVII (1959), 303–17. An analysis of what the *comedia* is and what makes it different from other manifestations of drama.

WADE, GERALD E. "The Interpretation of the *Comedia*," *Bulletin of the Comediantes*, XI, no. 1 (Spring, 1959), 1–6. A study that suggests the difficulty for moderns of getting inside the mind of the seventeenth-century playwright.

WILSON, MARGARET. *Spanish Drama of the Golden Age* (Oxford: Pergamon Press, 1969). A very good introduction, the only one of its kind in English, to the *comedia* and its chief representatives.

5. Staging of the *Comedia*

RENNERT, HUGO A. *The Spanish Stage in the Time of Lope de Vega* (New York: The Hispanic Society of America, 1909, and reprinted, without the list of actors and actresses, by Dover Publications, Inc., New York, 1963). A detailed account of the theater in the time of Alarcón.

SHERGOLD, N. D. *A History of the Spanish Stage* (Oxford: Clarendon Press, 1967). An exhaustive study of theaters and staging from Medieval times to the end of the seventeenth century.

6. The *Gracioso*

LEY, CHARLES DAVID. *El gracioso en el teatro de la península (siglos XVI-XVII)* (Madrid: Revista de Occidente, 1954). A rapid, somewhat superficial, survey of various *graciosos* of the Spanish theater.

7. The Honor Theme

CASTRO, AMÉRICO. "Algunas observaciones acerca del concepto del honor en los siglos XVI y XVII," in *Revista de Filología Española*, III (1916), 1–50, 357–86. A résumé of comments on honor by various critics as well as a study of the concept of honor based on numerous citations in various *comedias*.

JONES, C. A. "*Honor* in Spanish Golden Age Drama: Its Relation to Real Life and Morals," in *Bulletin of Hispanic Studies*, XXXV (1958), pp. 199–210. A realistic effort to put the conventional honor code of the *comedia* in its proper perspective.

JONES, C. A. "Spanish Honour as Historical Phenomenon, Convention and Artistic Motive," in *Hispanic Review*, XXXIII (Philadelphia, 1965), 32–39. Although concentrating on Calderón, the author shows how honor is used as a dramatic device.

STUART, DONALD C. "Honor in the Spanish Drama," in *Romanic Review*, I (New York, 1910), pp. 247–58, 357–66. A brief history of possible origins of the honor theme in the *comedia*.

8. Magic in the *Comedia*

PAVIA, MARIO N. *Drama of the Siglo de Oro, a Study of Magic, Witchcraft, and Other Occult Beliefs* (New York: Hispanic Institute in the United States, 1959). A survey of beliefs and practices of magic, with references to many plays of the Golden Age.

9. Versification

CLARKE, DOROTHY C. "A Chronological Sketch of Castilian Versification Together with a List of its Metric Terms," in *University of California Publications in Modern Philology*, XXXIV (Berkeley, 1952), no. 3, 279–382. Contains a list of definitions of the various types of strophe to be found in the *comedia*.

10. Histories of Spain

ATKINSON, WILLIAM C. *A History of Spain and Portugal* (London: Penguin Books, 1960). A rapid survey of Spanish and Portuguese history; the political decline of Spain during Alarcón's lifetime is set forth in Chapter 10.

DAVIES, H. TREVOR. *The Golden Century of Spain* (London: Macmillan and Company, Ltd., 1939). This with the same author's *Spain in Decline*, 1621–1700 (London: Macmillan and Company, Ltd., 1957) will serve the reader only of English as a good introduction to the Spain just before, during, and after Alarcón's existence.

HUME, MARTIN. *The Court of Philip IV* (London: Eveleigh Nash and Grayson, Ltd., n.d.). Chapters II and III deal, respectively, with the death of the Count of Villamediana and the visit of Charles, Prince of Wales, later Charles I, with which events Alarcón had some connection.

Index

The asterisk (*) indicates a character in a literary work (I am indebted to Professor John C. Dowling for this suggestion). Works by, or attributed to, Alarcón are indexed under the English translation of the title, with a cross reference under the Spanish title. All other literary and reference works are indexed under the original title, with translation and name of author; where no name is given, the work is anonymous.